Unleash
Your
PSYCHIC
POWERS

Unleash Your PSYCHIC POWERS

DR. BRUCE GOLDBERG

Sterling Publishing Co., Inc.
New York

NOTE TO THE READER

This book does not attempt to prescribe for or treat psychological or medical problems. If you have significant difficulties in your life, it is highly recommended that you seek the appropriate health practitioner.

Drawings on pages 34, 44, and 70 by Chad Wallace

Library of Congress Cataloging-in-Publication Data Available

10 9 8 7 6 5 4 3 2 1

Published by Sterling Publishing Company, Inc.
387 Park Avenue South, New York, N.Y. 10016
© 1997 by Bruce Goldberg
Distributed in Canada by Sterling Publishing
℅ Canadian Manda Group, One Atlantic Avenue, Suite 105
Toronto, Ontario, Canada M6K 3E7
Distributed in Great Britain and Europe by Cassell PLC
Wellington House, 125 Strand, London WC2R 0BB, England
Distributed in Australia by Capricorn Link (Australia) Pty Ltd.
P.O. Box 6651, Baulkham Hills, Business Centre, NSW 2153, Australia
Manufactured in the United States of America
All rights reserved

Sterling ISBN 0-8069-9723-0

Contents

INTRODUCTION

CONSIDER FOR A MOMENT that you require information about the future. It may involve a critical decision about your health, marriage, career, or a family member. Now imagine going to a quiet place and in a few minutes feeling completely relaxed and asking your Higher Self for the information necessary to make this decision or deal with this crisis.

A short time later you return to your quiet place and quickly relax. Once again you request information from your Higher Self and are presented with data instructing you how to proceed. This results in a stress-free decision for you that affects you and others around you positively.

This book is all about psychic development. You will be able to accomplish this decision-making ability routinely and with just about any goal. Everyone has psychic potential, but unfortunately most people have been programmed to think they don't.

Most people assume they lack psychic abilities because they were not born with them. Psychic talents are just like any other skills. They can be developed.

You may naturally have an affinity for certain techniques and not others. Some people are more adept at sports, others at creative or intellectual activities. It is not necessary for you to master equally every type of psychic ability. Dozens of exercises in this book will assist you in finding your psychic niche.

Eliminate the term "not psychic" from your vocabulary. Only by focusing on your own particular psychic expression will you facilitate the development of your psychic abilities. If you cannot do something that your friends or family can, do you consider yourself less sane? Of course you don't. Psychic gifts are similar. Some you will exhibit, while others may not come easily to you and these you may decide to ignore.

Another purpose of this book is to assist you in finding where your psychic talents are. By concentrating, studying, and trial and error, you will develop your psychic ability. This will open up a whole new and rewarding world to explore, but it must be done with discipline, patience, and the proper motivation.

The exercises presented in this book are designed to open up your channels of communication with your sixth sense. It may be that you access your natural psychic talents through your bodily sensations, hunches, feelings, or intuition. The purpose of this book is to assist you in your psychic development—to maximize your ability to perceive auras, hear voices, and see images, as an expression of your psychic awareness and spiritual growth.

You will learn to center yourself, relax, enter trance states, and channel communication from the "other side." You will also be guided in protection and healing techniques. These will assist you in your own spiritual growth and will create a more lasting and positive effect on others.

HOW TO USE THIS BOOK

This book contains dozens of exercises specifically designed to train you to increase your psychic development. It doesn't matter what your background is.

You can accept or reject any of the principles and concepts presented here. Empowerment is vital. I stress that in my hypnotherapy practice and in my personal life as well. If you become rigid and stuck in your views, you become trapped by your beliefs. You are no longer empowered because you are no longer free.

Always use your judgment and free will in trying these exercises. Use the ones you feel comfortable with and ignore the others. These exercises are all perfectly safe and have been tested for over 20 years. Or create your own exercises from these models or as directed by your own Higher Self.

Read each exercise through to become familiar with it. Use the relaxation techniques given or your own, center yourself, apply protection, and practice the exercises. You may practice alone or with others. Feel free to make tapes of these exercises. Read the scripts slowly and leave enough space on your tape to experience each part of the procedure.

If you experience difficulty with an exercise, do not become frustrated. Some techniques are quite advanced and you may not be ready for all of them. At another time, return to the ones you could not successfully work with. Your own Higher Self will direct you in this respect.

Practice these trance states when you have time and when you are relaxed. Be patient. It takes time to master trance states and to become accustomed to this new and wonderful world. No one way is *the* right way to experience a trance. Your body may feel light, or it may feel heavy; you may feel as if you are dreaming; your eyelids may flutter; or your body can become cooler or warmer. All these possible responses are perfectly safe.

Your initial practice sessions should as be as long as you need, since you are unfamiliar with the techniques. As you become more proficient, you will be able to shorten these sessions. Some days nothing may seem to work. Try not to become discouraged. Remember, other days will be more fruitful. Always work at your own pace and with an open mind.

Any image or experience that you find disconcerting can be terminated merely by blinking your eyes and saying, "Go in peace." By then opening your eyes, the image or sensation will disappear and you will return instantly to your normal waking state. Remember, you will always be protected by the white light, which represents your Higher Self and is always with you.

Sometimes you will feel a surge of energy after practicing an exercise. This can interfere with your normal sleep cycle. To drain excess energy simply shake your hands and place them palms-down on the floor to ground them. You can then visualize the energy draining off your aura (the electromagnetic energy field that surrounds your physical body and that is a component of the soul's energy) and being transferred to the floor. This effort can also be achieved by washing your hands in cold water.

How do you get to Carnegie Hall? The answer is practice, practice, and more practice. The same holds true with psychic development.

CHAPTER 1

WHAT IS PSYCHIC DEVELOPMENT?

THE GREEKS CALLED the soul *psychikes* (English, "psyche"). The term refers to aspects of our being beyond the known physical world. To be psychic is to receive information or sensations from sources other than the five senses. Sixth sense perception is perfectly normal and everyone is capable of exhibiting this psychic gift.

This inner sense, or sixth sense, is more readily seen among primitive peoples than in modern man. Shamans are the best example, as the tradition of shamans has been around for at least 50,000 years. These medicine men and women were skilled in magic and they used herbs, plants, and psychic energy for healing. Shamans had to endure rigorous tests before earning the right to practice their craft.

Intuition is a basic form of a natural psychic gift. An example of intuition would be an insight that allows you to solve a problem or be creative in some way. You "tune in" and listen to your Higher Self, even though you may not realize it. It is the interaction between you and the universe that accounts for psychic talent and allows for an unlimited expansion of mind.

Everyone is psychic. By increasing your ability to tap into this dimension and receive data and experiences from your Higher Self, you can maximize your psychic gifts. Anyone can develop his psychic abilities, not just those people who are born with these abilities well developed already.

Professional psychics use different methods to access information. Some have a deceased relative, a guide, or an angel who imparts information to them that they would otherwise find unobtainable. Others tap into a universal energy (collective unconscious) for assistance.

When a psychic receives information from another entity or energy source, the psychic is referred to as a *medium*. A psychic who hears information is called *clairaudient,* and one who sees an image, *clairvoyant* .

Divination is the term for foretelling the future by interpreting symbolic representations. Runes, I Ching, Tarot cards, palmistry, and tea leaves are examples of divination. Psychics access the Higher Self to interpret these symbols properly.

Regardless of the method, whenever you obtain information about the past, present, or future through means not part of your five senses, you are functioning as a psychic. A common definition of a psychic is a person who, while acting as a medium, is able to extract previously unknown information and predict future occurrences.

One of the greatest obstacles to psychic development is negativity. Low self-image, a difficult relationship, depression, and obsessive thoughts will distract you from your natural ability to access your Higher Self. I will shortly present an exercise to help prepare you for your initial steps towards psychic development and help you overcome obstacles.

It's easy to overlook the obvious. You probably forget about many examples of psychic energy, such as thinking of someone and immediately receiving a call from that person, sensing a problem with the baby in another room and intervening quickly enough to avert a major difficulty. And sudden changes in plans can avert tragedy. These are but a few examples.

Again, psychic energy is not available only to a select group. Everyone possesses it. Psychic development merely involves removing the obstacles and freeing the subconscious mind to tap into the Higher Self and channel this energy.

Once you clear the path of negativity and open yourself up to receive this energy, you will experience your psychic powers. Be patient and diligent in practicing the many exercises presented, for as you master each step you are bringing yourself closer to your goal of psychic development.

I do not believe that psychic gifts are inherited. No gene exists for psychic abilities. These powers are part of the soul or subconscious mind. The soul is electromagnetic energy (equivalent to a radio or television signal). You use this energy to receive and transmit psychic information. Since everyone has a soul, these psychic gifts are a part of all of us.

By developing your psychic abilities you will also become more emotionally sensitive to others and more creative. Psychics are often referred to as "sensitives." By expanding your psychic awareness you will be able to sense the obstacles and opportunities projected by yourself and others. This places on you a great responsibility. I cover this in the psychic ethics section of this book.

Your own natural tendencies toward optimism or pessimism may affect the reading you give others. Try to be objective. If you can't separate your personal agenda from your role as a psychic, either seek therapy or do not read for others.

The greatest benefit a psychic can give a subject is new information to help understand the causes of a problem. This can help a subject decide whether and how to change. The choice is always the subject's.

Before practicing any of the more involved psychic development exercises, learn to relax your body and mind. This simple breathing exercise never fails to calm both:

Breathe in while counting to four. Hold your breath for a count of four, then breathe out counting to four.

Breathe in while counting to eight. Hold your breath for a count of eight, then breathe out counting to eight.

Breathe in while counting to ten. Hold your breath for a count of ten, then breathe out counting to ten.

Now breathe normally for one minute and repeat the exercise.

◆　◆　◆　◆　◆

A PRELIMINARY EXERCISE IN PSYCHIC DEVELOPMENT

This basic exercise involves thinking about another person. It should be someone you are not emotionally close to, a relative stranger. This person could be a neighbor, co-worker, or cashier at the supermarket. All you need to do is maintain a conscious image of this person and block out all thoughts about yourself and anyone else while you practice this exercise.

Lie down on a couch or bed or get comfortable in a chair. Take a deep breath and hold it to the count of six, then let it out slowly. Do this again and concentrate on a mental image of the person. Focus on your third eye (the area between the eyebrows and at the top of your nose).

Visualize the person expressing different emotions. See the person cry, laugh, and look very serious. Try to hear the person expressing these emotions. As you do this, hold the mental image of each expression for a moment.

Try to feel the person's energy. How does it feel? Now relate to the person's outlook on life. Is this person happy or sad? Is the person content? What does this person aspire to in life?

Now imagine a white light surrounding the mental image of this person and close your third eye.

Did you notice a difference in your perception of this person? Focus on how you feel and how you relate to this person.

◆　◆　◆　◆　◆

As you complete this exercise, spend a few minutes writing down your impressions in a psychic journal. Do not allow your critical and analytical conscious mind to interfere with your thoughts. Keep this journal and use it with the other exercises in this book. Date your entry and note any difficulties that might have affected your ability to receive data.

This exercise has two main functions. First, it detaches you from your conscious mind and allows you to access your subconscious, Higher Self. It also gives you the opportunity to focus on someone you do not know. And second, it introduces you to the concept of tuning in to the vibratory force or energy (aura) surrounding another person. Finally, the white light in this exercise presents you with the protection technique that will be developed further in this book.

PSYCHIC ETHICS

You must always acknowledge universal laws as you expand your psychic skills. As you develop these abilities they will increase in power. However, with such power comes responsibility.

The energy you send out always comes back to you. When you send out love, you get love in return. If you attempt to hurt or manipulate others, you may succeed initially but you will have to pay back this energy misuse down the road.

The more you develop your psychic powers, the greater your responsibility to see that they are used properly. Psychic gifts must always be used in a non-violent and loving way.

You may be tempted to use your newly developed psychic powers to seek vengeance on someone who has wronged you. Do not give in to this temptation. The following examples will help clarify the principles of psychic ethics:

1. You are lonely and desire a partner. Someone you know appeals to you, but this person has not expressed interest in you. Should you send out energy to this person to encourage attraction? Absolutely not. This would be manipulative. It is never permissible to use psychic abilities without permission. A better solution would be to visualize yourself with a partner and let the universe create the opportunity.

2. A job interview is scheduled and you desperately need this position. Should you use your psychic skills to direct the interviewer to hire you? Again, doing so would be manipulative and is totally unacceptable. A permissible way to deal with the situation would be to enter into a trance and project the best possible energy for yourself to this interviewer. If you know the interviewer's name, you may project yourself on the astral plane and present your case. Just don't attempt to be manipulative.

3. You are in a relationship but are having communication problems. Is it acceptable to project your energy to mold your partner into the kind of person you want? No, of course not. What you can do is a visu-

alization exercise in which you see both yourself and your partner communicating better. In addition, you might want to focus on yourself and see yourself becoming more tolerant, patient, and calmer in dealing with your partner.

4. A friend of yours is ill. Can you send healing energy? You must obtain your friend's permission first. Acting on your own, even though you mean well, is an invasion of other people's psychic space. A better solution would be to call your friend and ask permission to project positive, healing energy.

CHAPTER 2

YOUR PSYCHIC STYLE

EVERYONE'S PSYCHIC STYLE is unique. The more you know about yourself and your own particular style, the more proficient you will be at developing your psychic abilities. In the end only you can best determine and increase your psychic gift.

There is no one right way to develop psychic talents. Some methods are simply easier and more efficient than others. Everyone has a natural psychic orientation. Yours may be toward precognition or perhaps clairvoyance. It is important to note that people tend to obtain from psychic abilities what they strive for. So, it is always to your advantage to aim high.

This chapter discusses the four main psychic styles. You can determine the one you have through a simple exercise. It is possible to be a mixture of two or more types, but one category is more likely to describe your style.

This exercise is to be fun. Do not pressure yourself. It will not determine your psychic fate for eternity. Take as much time as you like with the exercise. There is nothing wrong with repeating it several times to confirm your psychic style.

AN EXERCISE TO FIND YOUR PSYCHIC STYLE

For this procedure you will require a large sheet of paper and a box of crayons or colored magic markers. Do this exercise in a quiet place at a time when you won't be disturbed. The purpose is to expand your consciousness and determine your psychic style.

Read the word lists and copy down on paper words in any category that attract you and that appear to represent your personality and interests. Draw a circle and place one to three words in this circle. Now select a crayon or marker and color in this circle with a color that you feel applies.

FLOWING	RECEPTIVE	ABSTRACT	ACTIVE
instructive	nurturing	reformist	ethical
secluded	moody	eccentric	moral
subtle	food-oriented	intuitive	lucky
dreamlike	cautious	detached	foreign
hidden	child-loving	humanitarian	benevolent
movielike	feeling	tolerant	spiritually seeking
compassionate	traditional	communicative	philosophical
universally loving	sympathetic	cooperative	just
inspired	subconscious	breakthrough	enthusiastic
visionary	passive	experimental	athletic
artistic	sensitive	nontraditional	generous
aesthetic	nostalgic	unusual	farsighted
spiritual	intuitive	awakening	independent
intense	protective	free	honorable
mind-altering	reflective	broad-minded	charitable
musical	security-oriented	mental	optimistic
idealistic	accumulating	inventive	outgoing
sensitive	changeable	revolutionary	travel-minded
creative	materialistic	liberal	horizon-broadening
benevolent	receptive	insightful	expansive

It is critical that you not analyze your actions. Let your subconscious direct your choices. When you complete one circle, continue reviewing the word lists and repeat this procedure. Group these circles any way you wish. It is not unusual to favor certain colors and choose some much more than others. Let your subconscious guide your choices and actions.

There are no maximum or minimum numbers of words or circles. Choose as few or as many words as you like, and arrange circles as you please. Do not try to figure out a system or symbolism. Just have fun. When you have finished, meditate on your work for a few minutes. View what you completed as if you were appreciating a painting in a museum. Perceive it as a whole, but do not analyze any of the components. Is there a pattern to your choice?

After you have done this, take a clean sheet of paper and divide it into four columns, one for each of the psychic styles: flowing, receptive, abstract, and active. Add up the number of words in each category that appear on your completed drawing. Write that number in the appropriate column on the clean sheet of paper.

The category with the highest number is your psychic style. If two or more categories represent your highest number, you are a combination of these types. Each psychic style is characterized by a preference for certain colors. This may assist you in deciding which style best fits you.

Read the descriptions of the four psychic styles carefully. Only you can decide which one represents you.

THE FLOWING STYLE

These people are natural psychics. They are tuned in to feelings of others and themselves. Flowing types are very imaginative and often feel drained because they pick up negativity from all around them. People tend to consider flowing types strange. Flowing types tend to be greatly misunderstood. Flowing types receive and send energy spontaneously and know things intuitively but are unaware of the source of this knowledge.

Dreamers and mystics fit into this category. Such people find it difficult to verbalize their experiences, and often say, "I just know." Flowing types need to be grounded and, more often than not, cannot handle their gift without its interfering with their lives. This is the most accurate of psychic styles.

Flowing types are often professional psychics. They are creative and artistic and commonly become actors or other type of entertainers. These souls frequent the healing arts and may enter psychology or medicine. Moss-green, sky-blue, pale orange, pink, banana-yellow, lilac, and other soft pastel colors characterize their style.

THE RECEPTIVE STYLE

This category is far more grounded. Receptive types tend to feel sensations prior to receiving psychic information. Tingly sensations, "gut feelings," goose bumps, and headaches are common examples. Receptive types make excellent counselors and healers and are better receivers than senders of psychic energy. Receptive psychics distrust intuitions that are not accompanied by sensations. They are thorough, good listeners, and very patient.

The receptive mode is very conservative. Receptive psychics stay in their safety zone and often need to open themselves up in order to expand their horizons. They can become entrenched in a "psychic rut" and experience frustration. If you are this type, learn to trust your Higher Self. This will help you expand your psychic abilities.

Receptive psychics are real "karmic capitalists" and often cash in on their talents. Muted colors, such as mustard-yellow, forest-green, burgundy, and pumpkin-orange characterize this style.

THE ABSTRACT STYLE

Abstract types are very unpredictable. They are continually shifting and changing their orientation. An abstract-style psychic constantly asks "What if...?" For abstract types, going inward for answers is as natural as breathing. There are no limitations or concepts too far-fetched for this category.

If you are an abstract type you are probably quite adept at verbalizing your psychic experiences. You are probably tuned in visually and have clairvoyant visions regularly. You are emotionally detached and often fail to make concrete connections in your daily life.

One of the main problems of an abstract receiver is the tendency toward becoming intellectually involved with psychic gifts, but failing to make practical applications of this knowledge. Thinkers and scientists (including absent-minded professors) are examples of this type.

Shocking and unusual colors characterize the abstract category. Abstract types like green, electric blue, white, tangerine, violet, and black as their colors.

THE ACTIVE STYLE

This is a most enthusiastic and excitable type. The active psychic is attracted to new experiences. Active types are quick and spontaneous. Most of the time these psychics initiate contact. They are better senders than receivers. Active types are impatient and like to work alone.

Active types tend to be depressed, especially if they are not receiving their usual quota of insightful flashes. This category is represented by performers and athletes. Their colors are bright hues such as lime-green, lemon-yellow, orange, and fire engine–red.

The main advantage in ascertaining your psychic style is that you can better take advantage of your psychic gifts and maximize your skills. If, for example, you are a natural receiver, then you will learn to trust your intuition, your "gut feelings," and your instinct.

Your psychic style functions like a television tower and accompanying satellite dish. It will help you fine-tune your talents and point out your strengths and weaknesses so you can better send and receive your psychic energy and that of others.

YOUR RELAXATION STYLE

Now that you have determined your psychic style, I am going to present two different methods of relaxation–meditation and self-hypnosis. Try each of these basic exercises and decide which style you prefer. You can then continue practicing this style as I present other exercises throughout this book.

There is no particular advantage to one over the other. Use either or both to facilitate your psychic development.

Your own motivation is the key to the success of this approach. The techniques are actually quite simple and anyone can apply them. You must truly want to accomplish these goals or else nothing will avail.

Over the years I have found that using cassette tapes gives great results with hypnosis and meditation. The scripts in this chapter can be used for making tapes.

When a script indicates New Age music, use whatever music you like. However, you will find metaphysical music ideal for these experiences. Professionally recorded tapes are also suitable.

INSTRUCTIONS FOR MEDITATION SCRIPTS

Do not feel you must use these scripts word for word. Your Higher Self directs your meditation. Feel free to amplify and expand on the scripts. Allow your Higher Self to edit the scripts and personalize them for you.

Meditate once or twice a day, in 15- to 20-minute sessions. It is generally considered best to meditate before lunch or before dinner, although practice in the morning may provide a relaxing start for the entire day.

Four components of successful meditation are:

1. a quiet environment.

2. a mental device.

3. a passive attitude.

4. a comfortable position.

When you access the Higher Self (superconscious mind) you will observe the following:

1. a positive mood (tranquility, peace of mind).

2. an experience of unity or oneness with the environment, what the ancients called the joining of microcosm (man) with macrocosm (universe).

3. an inability to describe the experience in words.

4. an alteration in time/space relationships.

5. an enhanced sense of reality and meaning.

Ancient Hindu and Zen scriptures on meditation point out that it is far more important to *attempt* to achieve the Higher Self than it is to actually reach that state. By taking time out to meditate, you make a conscious effort to improve your health. This effect, by definition, is the opposite of the behavior pattern that leads to excessive stress. Conscious attention to meditation will remove much of the competitive component of this process.

GENERAL MEDITATION

Focus all your attention on your breath. Concentrate on the mechanics of breathing. Note how the breath comes and goes. As the breath enters and leaves the nostrils, feel the expansion and contraction of the lungs.

Focus on the awareness of breathing. Remove all other thoughts and feelings from your awareness.

Observe this natural life process. Do not try to change it. Merely be with it.

Let yourself receive the changing sensations that accompany this process.

As you inhale and exhale, one breath at a time, let it happen by itself. If it is deep, let it be deep. If it is slow, let it be slow. If it is shallow, let it be shallow.

If you sense that your mind is interfering with this process, just focus on the inhalation and exhalation. Be one with your breath. Nothing else matters.

Observe the uniqueness of each breath. Observe, don't analyze. Note the changing sensations. Be one with your breath.

Ignore all other functions of the body. Remove all thoughts from your mind. You are the breath. Be one with your breath. *Egyptians*

You are now floating with the universe. As the wind carries a feather, you are being carried by your breath.

Notice how the distracting thoughts fade. How they become meaningless. All that matters is that you breathe. You are your breath. Be one with your breath.

Let go of your body. Feel as if you have no body. You are weightless, as is your breath.

You are floating in the universe. You are at peace with the universe. You are one with the universe.

Notice how relaxed you are, now that you are free of the confines of your body. You are totally one with the universe.

There is nowhere to go. Nobody is expecting you. You have no schedule or deadline.

You are free. Enjoy this moment, for you are one with the universe.

Be quiet. Do not cough or make any movement or sound. Just be still and merge with the universe. You are consciousness.

Let go of all fear and doubt. Let go of all thoughts. Do not try to control your feelings. Just be free and one with your consciousness.

You have no body. You have no limitations. You are one with your consciousness. You are one with the universe.

Let each moment occur by itself. Observe it and enjoy these intervals of time. Do not resist this merging with your consciousness.

You are now nothing but consciousness. You are the universe.

(Play New Age music for 15 minutes.)

Now it is time to return to your body. Again, concentrate on your breath. Now note the other functions of your body. Slowly open your eyes and do what you feel is important at this time.

◆   ◆   ◆   ◆   ◆

HYPNOSIS

Hypnosis is pleasant. It is a state of deep concentration. The conscious mind is relatively weak. It vacillates continuously and will create an endless round of excuses why you should not bother getting something done, such as developing your psychic abilities. The conscious mind lacks the kind of stabilizing force that the subconscious possesses.

The subconscious mind can best be influenced in a passive or relaxed state, such as in hypnosis. This restful quieting of the mind cleanses it, opening it to pure, more elevated thoughts from your psychic energy source, the Higher Self. Hypnosis builds both mental vigor and enthusiasm because it removes all fear and the negative thoughts that act as roadblocks to energy, inspiration, and accomplishment.

I suggest that two periods a day be put aside to train your subconscious mind. These need to be only 10 minutes each. The best time is very early in the morning, shortly after awakening. The other can be at any convenient time during the day. Do not practice hypnosis before bedtime unless you are having difficulty falling asleep.

A HYPNOSIS EXERCISE

Go into a room and close the door to shut out distracting sounds. Lie down on a bed or couch and relax as well as you can for about two to five minutes. Your mind and body both will tend to relax as you lie inert, and this passive state will open a door that swings its way to the subconscious mind. As you rest quietly, close your eyes and think of a warm, relaxed feeling.

Focus all your attention on the muscles in the toes of both your feet. Imagine this warm, relaxed feeling spreading and surrounding the muscles of your toes, moving to the backs of both feet and to your heels and ankles. Now imagine this warm feeling moving up the calf muscles of both your legs to your kneecaps and into the thigh muscles, meeting at the hip bone.

This warm, relaxing feeling is moving up your backbone to the middle of your back, surrounding the shoulder blades and moving into the back of the neck.

This warm, relaxing feeling is now moving into the fingers of both hands, just as it did with the toes. The feeling now spreads into the back of both hands, into palms, wrists, forearms, elbows, shoulders, and neck, relaxing each and every muscle along its path.

This warm, relaxing feeling now moves into the intestines, stomach, chest, and neck muscles.

This warm, relaxing feeling now moves into the back of your head, scalp, and all the way to the forehead. Now, your facial muscles are relaxed; now your eyes (which are closed), the bridge of your nose, your jaws (the upper and lower teeth are separated), chin, earlobes, and neck. Now each and every muscle in your entire body is completely relaxed.

When you feel relaxed throughout your body or feel a heaviness in your arms and legs, you have reached the light stages of hypnosis.

◆　◆　◆　◆　◆

Continue this exercise for several days, then progress to the next section, which is more advanced. The instructions are made a part of the mental dialogue that you will be thinking to yourself. Read it over two or three times to commit the general idea to your memory rather than trying to remember it word for word. I recommend making tapes of these scripts.

To go deeper into hypnosis can be accomplished in a number of ways. One of the more common is to imagine a very pleasant and soothing scene, such as a green valley that you are looking down into from a mountaintop. Watch a lazy brook meander its way through the valley and relax more and more as you watch its slow movements.

Another way is to imagine yourself descending a flight of stairs very slowly. Think, as you wend down the ancient stone stairwell, that you are going deeper and deeper with each step. The following script can be used to deepen the hypnotic trance state:

I want you to imagine that you are standing on the fifth floor of a large department store and that you are just stepping into the elevator to descend to street level. And as you go down and as the elevator door opens and closes as you arrive at each floor, you will become more and more deeply relaxed and your sleep will become deeper and deeper.

The doors are closing now and you are beginning to sink slowly downward.

The elevator stops at the fourth floor. Several people get out, two more get in, and the doors close again; and already you are becoming more and more deeply relaxed, more and more deeply asleep.

And as you sink to the third floor and stop, the doors open and close again. You are relaxing more and more, and your sleep is becoming deeper and deeper.

You slowly sink down to the second floor. One or two people get out and several get in. And as they do so, you are feeling much more deeply relaxed, much more deeply asleep.

You travel down once again to the first floor. The doors open and close but nobody gets in or out. You have become still more deeply relaxed and your sleep still deeper and deeper. You are more and more deeply asleep…more and more deeply asleep.

You travel down further and further until the elevator stops at last at street level. The doors open and everybody gets out.

But you do not get out. You decide to go still deeper and descend to the basement.

The elevator doors close again. Down you go, down and down, deeper and deeper. And as you arrive at the basement, you are feeling twice as deeply and comfortably relaxed, twice as deeply asleep.

◆   ◆   ◆   ◆   ◆

As you develop skill with your own mind, you will be able to go into a trance much more quickly. Even surroundings that used to be too distracting to handle will now be tolerable for practicing self-hypnosis.

Do the following exercise after your meditation or after relaxing prior to your self-hypnosis relaxation preparation. This is a basic psychic-development visualization and mind-expanding technique.

Imagine yourself taking the form of an eagle. You are flying several hundred feet above the earth, completely free and uninhibited. Feel yourself soaring, gliding, climbing upward to your Higher Self. Floating freely in the air, you can observe the world unfolding below you. See the colors of the planet, the blues and greens, the earth tones.

Sense the majesty of the heavens and the panorama of the living universe. Soar and glide to the rhythm of life. Ride the wind and soar higher and higher. You have freed yourself from the earthly bonds that once shackled your mind to convention, self-doubt, and confusion. Feel the quiet radiance of life surrounding you; hear the harmony that is you in tune with creation. Be still, observe, and know.

Glide upward—ever upward—toward understanding, toward light, and toward beauty. Beauty surrounds you in this sanctity of space. This is where other worlds exist beyond the confines of your everyday mind. Just as a seed contains the promise of fulfillment, your mind already contains the promise of greater gifts.

As you let go of fixed ideas, doubts, and other negative influences, you open the way for love, patience, and gentleness. Your Higher Self guides you to enjoy the rewards of your new reality.

Be receptive to the guidance of your Higher Self. Your Higher Self guides you and protects you, even when you are not consciously aware of it. Grow in the silence of your spiritual self. See the white light all around you.

Be still and listen. Your Higher Self already knows your needs and guides you to live a clear new way each day. It will guide you to action by giving you gifts of the spirit.

When you talk with someone, listen—really listen—with your inner ear as well as your outer ears. You may hear things being said at the inner level that are not spoken at the outer levels. Listen also to your inner voice and respond to it.

When you see a person or an event, look—really look—and perceive it with your inner vision. See and understand the workings behind the scenes. Open yourself to all impressions; look deeper than the surface.

Now create a picture or vivid symbol of yourself using and applying your psychic gifts. Bring your accomplished ideals and goals together into a specific image. Visualize your goals as already accomplished.

Now slowly return from your upward flight. Return as a floating feather. Circle gently and land softly on the beach. Bring something positive and helpful back with you. Hear the waves and recall the thoughts, feelings, symbols, and ideas from your journey. You are developing your gifts and learning to use them daily as you open yourself up to information and psychic energy from your Higher Self.

CHAPTER 3

THE AURA

WE ALL HAVE an electromagnetic field of energy surrounding us known as the aura. The technique of Kirlian photography actually photographs the aura of plants, animals, and man.

Psychically the aura is perceived as a series of colors. Feel it by placing your hands near your body. The aura radiates light and vibrates constantly. It is said that even rocks have this aura.

Your aura is the outward extension of the soul's energy. It holds within the electromagnetic energy field a record of every event that has happened to you, including past-life experiences.

An inner center of colors shines through the electromagnetic field, and these colors are relatively easy to perceive psychically. These colors are pink/red, blue/green, blue, mauve, and yellow. They represent health, balance, and spirit energy.

The electromagnetic layer is closer to the body and reflects the colors of the inner center and the surrounding energy of the body. This electromagnetic layer is affected when the body is fatigued, distressed, or unbalanced. The normal strong and uniform glow of the electromagnetic layer can appear thin and weak under duress or illness. If you are excited and charged with energy, this layer glows brightly all around the physical body.

The aura is actually a complete record of the spiritual and physical status of the soul and its physical body. Each color has special meanings depending on where it is found and depending on its particular shade. We will discuss these meanings later on.

Some auras are thin and others are wide. What is most important psychically is the overall sense of awareness, the peace and the energy, not how large the aura appears.

Tune into the aura psychically by sensing its energy as colors, pictures, feelings, or thoughts. It is easier to perceive the aura from the waist up. Initially it is seen as a gray or white mist around the head. With a little practice the colors I alluded to earlier can be observed.

The aura may be seen psychically as an oval-shaped ring of light that either pulses or appears as a swirling pattern of several colored lights. Some people may not actually see this electromagnetic field, but will feel or otherwise sense it.

The aura is composed of seven interwoven rings of light and each component represents something else.

The seven aura rings are as follows:

1. Ring 1 represents physical health.

2. Ring 2 represents the emotions.

3. Ring 3 represents the intellect.

4. Ring 4 represents the subconscious, especially the imagination and intuition.

5. Ring 5 represents the Higher Self.

6. Rings 6 and 7 are not visible on most people and represent advanced cosmic aspects of the soul's energy.

We usually see the first ring when we psychically observe another's aura. Anyone can be trained to do this. Fortunately, it is not necessary to see or distinguish each of the five observable rings of the aura to obtain information about the person you are reading.

Spiritually evolved people have a clear and bright aura that tends to project further out than that of the average person. This is especially noticeable around the head. The halo of light around saints and masters, as artists have depicted throughout history, reflects this advanced aura. Several energy fields surround the body. Included among these are magnetic, sound, heat, electrical, and light.

Before sensing the aura psychically, it is important to clear your own aura. The following exercise is designed to assist you in clearing your aura:

Use one of the relaxation exercises previously given. Tell yourself you wish to clear your aura. Stand up and breathe in deeply. As you exhale, visualize a circle of energy in the form of a white light above your head. Sense this energy moving in a clockwise direction as it moves down your body.

All negativity is now being removed from your aura and sent to the ground beneath your feet, where it will be neutralized. Now take in a few deep breaths and relax.

◆　◆　◆　◆　◆

You are ready to clear the aura of someone you are about to read psychically. This exercise is designed to clear another person's aura.

Have your subject stand feet-apart and arms hanging loosely. Do not touch your subject, but do the following procedures approximately two inches (5 cm) from his or her skin surface:

With your thumbs touching and your hands spread out, move your hands from the top of your subject's head until you reach the floor. Remember not to touch your subject.

Now go back and repeat this procedure clockwise until you have encircled your subject. Last, do the arms, inner legs, and under each foot. Have your subject shake his or her body and sip some water. The aura is now cleansed.

◆　◆　◆　◆　◆

The next step is to begin sensing the electromagnetic layer next to the body. This is easy to see and is most commonly observed as a white glow. The following exercise will help you tune into this layer of the aura.

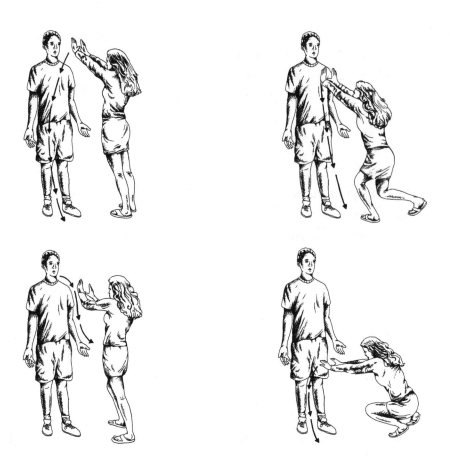

Relax and inwardly direct yourself toward seeing your subject's aura. Breathe gently while facing your subject and clear your mind. Do not stare, especially at the eyes. Look through or around your subject.

Place your attention around the head and shoulder region. As you defocus your eyes and gaze, a white glow will appear. If this glow is still present when you look away completely, it is an optical illusion and must be ignored. Only the glow surrounding a person is a true representation of the person's aura.

◆ ◆ ◆ ◆ ◆

AURA CLEARING

Practice this exercise several times with the same subject. The colors of the subject's aura will be seen as fluctuating, moving, fading, and deepening in no particular order. They appear as sunlight shining through stained glass. The head and shoulders are the easiest place to observe these colors. You will only see a momentary glow or flash of color, as they are constantly moving and changing.

The aura is self-contained. It has no holes. It does not leak or disappear. The energy field may release or absorb energy, but the total amount of energy it contains remains constant.

To facilitate your perception of colors, here are two recommended techniques:

Stare at a card that is green, mauve, blue/green, pink/red, yellow, or blue. These are the colors of the inner center of the astral body (a less material body that surrounds the physical body). When you can see this color with your eyes closed, quickly open your eyes and look at your subject's head. The color on the card will be superimposed on your subject's head. Do this exercise with each of the other colors.

You can use either light shining through stained glass, or colored light bulbs with your subject.

◆　◆　◆　◆　◆

Both exercises are meant merely for training and conditioning your mind to see colors. They are not meant to be used on a regular basis, just until you become proficient at seeing the aura.

Another exercise you can try is to relax yourself and sit in a comfortable chair. Stare at your own body, beginning with your fingers. See your own aura as you look at your hands and arms. Then look at your head in a mirror and use the gazing method described earlier.

◆　◆　◆　◆　◆

OTHER HINTS TO FACILITATE SEEING AURAS

Look at your subject with blurred eyes. It is best not to wear your glasses.

Relax yourself with meditation or hypnosis prior to observing auras.

Look at the head and shoulder region first.

Have your subject sit in front of a light-colored or white background. Ask your subject to close his eyes and to concentrate on sending you energy.

While your subject is concentrating, close your eyes and ask your Higher Self for assistance. Open your eyes and begin gazing at your subject's forehead. Occasionally close your eyes, as you may first see the outline of the aura when your eyes are closed.

Ask your subject to concentrate on shaping the aura into a peak at the top of his head. Your subject should also focus entirely on one color.

◆　◆　◆　◆　◆

The following exercise demonstrates how energy can be transferred from the aura of two people:

Have two people sit at a slight distance from each other. Each should relax, as should you, using the exercises previously described. Now ask both of them to concentrate on sending energy into the other's aura. Watch them closely, paying particular attention to the space between them. You will soon see their auras vibrating and expanding and eventually meeting. This may appear as a flash of light. Do not be concerned about cross-contamination (the light of each person's aura field meeting at the same point), as the aura energy of each person will return to its respective point of origin.

◆　◆　◆　◆　◆

Be patient with this advanced exercise. It often takes several attempts to be successful. The results depend on each person's ability to project energy and your talent to visualize this transfer.

Here is an exercise that is a diagnostic tool for healers:

Relax yourself and your subject, then slowly move your hands (thumbs touching and palms open) around the person's body. Do not touch, but remain about an inch (2.5 cm) away from the skin. Focus on your subject's energy and ask your Higher Self for assistance. Observe just how far away from your subject you can be and still perceive the aura. Some spots will feel warmer or cooler than others. Legs usually feel cooler and are harder to detect.

See if you can detect any disruptions in the flow of energy. Unusually warm or cool places indicate blocked energy. Ask if your subject has had, or is having, difficulties with that part of the body. Subjects often report sprains or backaches or even headaches at these hot or cold spots.

◆　◆　◆　◆　◆

THE MEANING OF AURA COLORS

There are many schools of thought about the psychic meaning of colors. Some colors affect the body because of their lower frequencies, while others influence the brain due to their higher frequencies. The following chart summarizes these effects:

PHYSICAL

Green, light blue	Restful
Red	Stimulating
Orange	Revitalizing

EMOTIONAL

Turquoise, sky blue	Restful
Orange	Stimulating
Peach	Revitalizing

MENTAL

Indigo	Restful
Yellow	Stimulating
Emerald green	Revitalizing

SPIRITUAL

Blue	Restful
Violet, purple	Stimulating
Gold	Revitalizing

Each color represents a certain light frequency and can be calming or stimulating, depending on the system. No one effect is guaranteed from a particular color. Responses depend on many factors in your own aura and the environment you live in.

For example, men and women traditionally respond differently to colors. Men tend to be more attracted to the red-orange range, whereas women tend to prefer the red-violet combination. Women most definitely tend to like pink, but this is not a color chosen by most men.

Here are the various colors you are likely to observe in auras and their generally accepted meanings:

COLOR	EFFECT
Indigo	Altered states of consciousness, integration, and purification. Too much of this color leads to depression.
Silver	A high degree of psychic development.
Red	This color represents pure energy and is subdivided as follows:
Basic red	Courage and strength
Brick red	Anger
Crimson	Loyalty
Deep red	Sensuality
Pink	Soothingness, optimism, and cheerfulness
Brown	This is a stabilizing, earthy, and grounding color.
Dull brown	Low energy
Gold	Intuition and knowing. This is a very spiritual color and amplifies psychic abilities.
Purple	Spiritual power. The deeper the purple, the greater the psychic significance.
Violet	Stimulates dream activity and psychic perception of past lives.
Blue	Intellectual development, creative expression, imagination, and idealism.
Orange	Optimism, vitality, joy, and a balance of the mental and physical. Often preferred by salespeople, speakers, promoters, and media personalities.
Yellow	Mental activity, wisdom, creativity, and emotions.
Yellow-gray	Fear
Green	Compassion, balance, growth, ingenuity, and a calming effect.
Pale green	Healing powers
Green-gray	Envy and pessimism
Black	Depression and death. This is rarely seen.
White	Purity and deep spirituality. White represents all the colors of the visible spectrum.

When you begin looking at subjects' auras, you will perceive a halo-shaped whitish or yellowish glow. Other colors will drift in and out with the subject's mood. One or two colors will tend to stand out. Allow the awareness and meaning of each color to arise from your inner self when you practice these exercises.

CHAPTER 4

PSYCHIC ENERGY

HOW PSYCHIC ENERGY WORKS

By developing your psychic abilities you are placing your soul's energy (aura) in contact with another's and establishing a connection. This connection is a flow of energy in both directions between you and this other person. This psychic energy is part of the soul and is self-replenishing.

You will need to switch down after practicing your psychic skills, especially when working with others. The two most vulnerable parts of your body are the nape of the neck and the center of the forehead. If you do not switch down, the continual flow of energy from others may leave you feeling overly energized and light-headed. You may also experience feelings of depression, irritability, lethargy, and apathy.

You may develop headaches and neck pains if you engage in physical activity, such as jogging, following your psychic exercises. The following exercise will help you to switch down after your psychic exercises and protect you from physical discomfort:

Stand with your elbows level with your shoulders and your feet slightly apart. Your palms should face inward and your hands should be level with the side of your head. Move your hands together directly in front of your forehead and slowly lower them. Raise your hands and arms back to the shoulder position and bring your palms together at the middle of your forehead. Now raise them, still held together, over the top of your head and down the nape of your neck and off at the shoulders. Lower your hands to your waist and pass them over each other. Last, stroke your body in a downward direction, brushing each leg and brushing under both feet; then shake your body.

◆　◆　◆　◆　◆

Another exercise to replenish your energy is as follows:

Hold your hands around a glass half filled with water that was boiled and has cooled. Hold the sides of the glass and focus your eyes on this water for 15 seconds. Sense the energy in the water and finally drink the water.

◆　◆　◆　◆　◆

Another technique for recharging yourself is as follows:

Stand relaxed and with your feet slightly apart. Stretch your arms out sideways just higher than your shoulders. Slowly bring your palms together, arms outstretched in front of you, and bring them to rest on your solar plexus, palms together and fingers pointing upward. Now stretch both arms out below the level of your shoulders and remain in this position for 15 seconds. Then bring your arms back again to your solar plexus, palms together and fingers pointing upward. Now stretch your arms out to your sides again, and then this time point your outstretched fingers downward toward the ground. Hold your hands in this position for 15 seconds. Now rest them once again on your solar plexus, fingers pointing upward. Hold them there for 30 seconds.

◆　◆　◆　◆　◆

At the end of the day you may feel especially drained. To wind down and prepare for bed, avoid watching television. Play soft music or New Age music. Lie down and sense colors and peaceful vibrations gently flowing all around your body. Slowly take a breath and feel your mind and body calming down. As you exhale, continue breathing rhythmically and visualize each and every part of your body relaxing.

This will quickly lead to natural sleep. If it does not immediately, repeat this exercise.

Always practice a grounding exercise before you attempt psychic techniques. Here is a simple exercise to assist you in stabilizing your energy:

> Stand with your feet firmly on the ground. Then breathe in deeply. Next, sit in a comfortable chair. Visualize the earth forming a cord, entering your feet, and moving all the way up your spine to the top of your head. Focus on a band of energy coming from the sky and entering this cord. As you sit, feel the energy from above neutralizing any negative effects of the earth's energy.

◆ ◆ ◆ ◆ ◆

AN EXERCISE TO ACCESS YOUR PSYCHIC ENERGY

To practice this exercise correctly, relax, breathe gently, and sit quietly. Ask your Higher Self for permission to access your psychic energy.

> Breathe deeply. Place both hands in front of your forehead, fingers pointing upward. Lift your hands upward and outward while continuing to breathe deeply. Place your hands on either side of your head, palms facing you. Say, "Om," while exhaling slowly. Bring your hands to rest in front of your neck with the fingers still pointing upward.

> Repeat this procedure and instead of having your hands end up in front of your neck, have them rest, facing downward, on your solar plexus, then in your lap.

> Finally, sit in this same position for two minutes and visualize warm energy and a white light surrounding your entire body. You have now tapped into your psychic energy.

> Breathe slowly and ask your Higher Self to disconnect you from your psychic energy to end this exercise. Open your eyes and touch a solid object near you as a ground. You are now free to do whatever you like without having to worry about continued exposure to your psychic energy.

◆ ◆ ◆ ◆ ◆

The next exercise is designed to balance your psychic energy with your physical body. Do not end the preceding exercise but continue with this one as follows:

Breathe slowly. Keep your hands palms-down in your lap. Focus your energy as a white light, and visualize it rising through your body from your toes to the top of your head.

This is your soul's energy. As you continue breathing rhythmically this white light will be joined by other colors. All during this time you are very relaxed and are experiencing a feeling of harmony, peace, and balance.

Stay in this state for between five and 10 minutes. End this trance immediately by opening your eyes if you feel a floating sensation or perceive yourself leaving your physical body. You are perfectly safe if you do exhibit an out-of-body experience (OBE), but that is not the purpose of this exercise.

This exercise is completed by asking your Higher Self to disconnect you from your psychic energy. Visualize the colors leaving the white light and the white light itself leaving your physical body from the top of your head. Open your eyes and pick up a solid object. You may also want to drink some water.

◆　◆　◆　◆　◆

You must be patient and conscientious in practicing these two exercises. Do not expect immediate results or try to rush them.

FOCUSING YOUR ENERGY

To tap into your psychic energy and maximize your psychic abilities requires you to focus your energy. This will not only improve your abilities, it will help you handle these procedures comfortably and with minimal drain to your body's physical energy.

The following exercise is designed to assist you in focusing:

Place a lit candle at eye level and sit in a chair within four feet (120 cm) of it. Make sure there are no drafts. Set a timer for 10 minutes and end this exercise when the timer sounds.

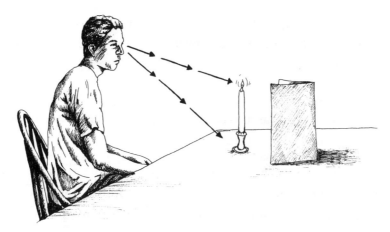

Relax and breathe deeply. Ask your Higher Self to assist you in projecting colors onto this candle flame. Concentrate on the color blue and mentally project that color onto the flickering candle flame. When you see the blue color, look away from the candle and begin again.

Stare at the candle flame once more, only this time focus on the color green and repeat this procedure.

◆　◆　◆　◆　◆

FOCUSING ON A CANDLE

Your conscious mind might tempt you with outside thoughts. Ignore these mental distractions and continue gazing at the candle flame. You cannot succeed with this exercise if you focus on outside thoughts. You must discipline yourself to deal only with the candle. Ignore any type of distraction in the room or your home.

In subsequent sessions you might want to raise or lower the flame with your mind as you develop your psychic powers.

Extinguish the candle and drink some water to complete this exercise. This exercise is very important, as it disciplines your mind to focus on only one thing at a time. When you work with someone else, or even alone, this training will pay great dividends psychically.

MEDITATION

I have previously presented a simple meditation exercise in Chapter 2. This technique is excellent for tapping into your psychic energy.

Meditation also functions to cleanse the mind of fears and to release creative and psychic energy. This connects your subconscious with the Higher Self.

Three main methods of meditation exist. These are presented as follows:

1. *Affirmations.* These are positive statements acknowledging your wisdom, health, and strength. These are repeated over and over while in a relaxed state.

Here are several affirmations that lend themselves easily to meditation: "All is One and I am One with All That Is." "I have found the inner harmony that flows through me and my body and mind." "A golden spirit flows through me and within that spirit I will live." "There is harmony of season and direction." "I know I am where I am supposed to be." "We all are one and the force that holds us together is love."

2. *Mantras.* Words or syllables whose sound and rhythm create an altered state of consciousness are known as mantras. These are chanted over and over again. "Om" is the most popular mantra.

3. *Breath Control.* This is achieved by exercises such as the general meditation exercise in Chapter 2.

Always sit in a comfortable position when meditating. Keep your back straight and your feet firmly on the floor. It is not necessary to use the lotus position (a cross-legged Yoga position), and most Westerners find this very uncomfortable and unnatural.

Tuck your chin in slightly and focus your concentration on the third eye (the point between your eyebrows). Take deep breaths and relax yourself. Choose one of the three methods described and focus on nothing else. If you find yourself thinking of other things, understand that this is your conscious mind's attempt to prevent you from growing spiritually. Ignore these distractions and return your focus to your chosen method of meditation. Do this exercise for 10 to 15 minutes before going on to the next exercise.

◆　◆　◆　◆　◆

Here are some hints about meditation:

1. Images you can focus on, such as a quiet lake, moonbeams across the water, a rose, and a flickering candle, work well.

2. For breathing techniques, watch your breath as it moves through your body. Note any feelings and sensations as you visualize your consciousness slowly moving from the top of your head all the way down to your feet. Do this for 15 minutes to half an hour.

3. Do not try to change things or analyze them while you meditate. Just become aware of them. As your meditation practice continues, you will find more space in your mind. That is, thoughts and images will intrude less frequently during your meditation. The habitual patterns may loosen. Do not become attached to the calmness or the peace you experience during meditation; just be aware of them as changing states of mind. Thoughts or images will probably always arise, but the periods of stillness will become longer. What will change is your ability to relate to whatever arises. It is possible to learn to be non-judgmental—neither praising nor condemning, but just being.

4. Whatever approach you use to initiate meditation will become easier with continued practice and patience.

CENTERING YOUR AWARENESS

You must clear your mind and relax in order to center your awareness. There are several ways to do this. The following exercises will facilitate centering in preparation for psychic development:

While breathing slowly, imagine that you are exhaling through a point about one inch (2.5 cm) below your navel.

Repeat the word "center" or use your meditation mantra.

Visualize extending your aura to the center of the earth.

Practice slow, deep breathing. The time you spend inhaling should equal that of exhaling. You can easily monitor this by counting.

Lengthening the exhalation phase of breathing is another good technique.

Imagine that you are blowing out a candle. Make the amount of time you exhale double your inhaling. This will center you quickly.

Another breathing technique is to inhale slowly through your nose, hold your breath, exhale slowly through your nose, and pause. Continue breathing in the same manner.

Inhale slowly through your nose, hold your breath as long as is comfortable, and then exhale slowly through your nose.

Inhale slowly through your nose to the count of four, hold your breath to the count of 12, and exhale slowly to the count of eight.

◆ ◆ ◆ ◆ ◆

CIRCLE OF PROTECTION

It is always wise to protect yourself before you practice psychic development, especially when you work with others. You have no idea what negativity people you are working with may be experiencing. Unless your are protected, you are particularly vulnerable to this negativity when you open yourself up psychically.

A circle of protection may be anything that suggests protection to you. Crystals, color, mirrors, sound, or light can be used. Most commonly white light is used for this protection. Some people use orange-, gold-, or silver-colored lights.

Stand while you do this protection exercise. Begin by surrounding yourself with a circle of light. This allows you to remain receptive and open without absorbing any negative energy. It's a good idea to use a circle if you are with a friend who is depressed and you don't want to pick up any negativity. You will find that as your sensitivity increases, so will your need for protection.

CIRCLE OF PROTECTION EXERCISES

Light three white candles. Sit or recline with the candles about 12 inches (30 cm) around you. Now relax and center yourself. Affirm to yourself: "I call upon the powers of the universe, all that is kind, loving, and good. I call especially on my spirit guides to be with me and add their energy to mine. I am surrounding myself with a beautiful circle of light, a shimmering white light. This light protects me from all negativity. Nothing can harm me now. I now release all negative energy from myself." Breathe deeply and exhale through your mouth as if you were blowing out a candle.

Stand with your feet firmly on the ground. Make sure the outsides of the feet are parallel. Shake your arms and legs. Breathe deeply and center yourself. Imagine a white light entering the top of your head and surrounding your entire body. See this light source resting six inches (15 cm) above your head and expanding your aura. Move this light down your entire body until you reach your feet.

Now imagine a second white light emanating from your heart and again permeating your entire body. See it, feel it, make it your reality. Coordinate your breathing with the expansion of your aura and the protection this white light affords your entire body and being.

◆　◆　◆　◆　◆

The next exercise will assist you in creating a positive mind-set for psychic experiences. Use usual images to create this pleasant and spiritual place. Always relax with a meditation or hypnosis technique first.

IMAGES TO USE FOR CREATING A POSITIVE MIND-SET

Ride in a crescent-shaped boat through a long, winding tunnel and come to rest in a quiet grotto.

Walk through a cool, damp forest to a clearing where you rest beside a gurgling spring.

Enter a cave in the side of a hill and wander down through the labyrinth of time until you reach a healing space, a calm space.

Walk down a long, winding staircase that leads to a river where a small boat is tied. Sail off in the boat, floating down the river until your boat washes ashore at the edge of a meadow.

Climb a long, winding path until you reach a cabin on the top of a mountain.

Fly on the back of a beautiful bird and land on the top of a mountain.

Ride a winged horse across the desert until you come to a cool oasis.

◆   ◆   ◆   ◆   ◆

Once you have mastered this simple technique, you can use this mind-set to:

1. Communicate with your Higher Self.

2. Remove creative or emotional blocks.

3. Control your dreams.

4. Meet your masters and guides.

5. Heal yourself.

6. Practice creative visualization and thought projection.

THE FLOW OF ENERGY

The universe is composed of energy. Einstein showed that energy can create matter, and matter can be converted back into energy. This energy is never lost; it is merely transformed from light to electricity to heat, and so on.

It's easy to forget that the energy in and around the physical body is identical to the energy found in the universe. For example, our subconscious (soul) is composed of electromagnetic radiation. This is the form of energy in radio and television signals.

The Chinese describe the phenomenon of the continual inward and outward flow of energy as the Yin and Yang principle. Yang (the male, aggressive) and Yin (the female, receptive) are components of the same energy. Life could not exist without both Yin and Yang. An excellent example is breathing. Inward movement of air (inhalation) and outward movement (exhalation) are both equally necessary to sustain life. Imbalance results from identifying too much with one form of this energy.

The universal energy is always available. You have all the energy you need. If you fill your mind with fears and problems, you block the flow of energy. If you focus your mind on the universal energy, it will flow freely through you. The amount of energy available to you is directly proportional to the universality of your motives. Fear, anger, greed, or envy limit the flow of your energy. When you are motivated by love and work towards the higher good, the energy available to you increases. The energy of the universe is limitless and is diminished only by your fears and learned limitations. Each time you give out energy, new energy flows into its place. It is only when you try to hoard the energy that the vital force is restricted. This is sometimes referred to as the universal law of supply and demand.

The following exercise will help you to experience this continual flow of psychic energy within your body:

Relax and stand up. Close your eyes and imagine that you are a pitcher of water. Bend slowly to the right as you imagine the water pouring out. Bend only as far as you can without losing your balance. Now move slowly back to an upright position, imagining that the pitcher is again filling with water. Now bend slowly to the left as you imagine the water pouring out. Bend only as far as you can without losing your balance. Once again move back to an upright position. Repeat these motions several times until you feel comfortable doing them.

◆　◆　◆　◆　◆

This next exercise will also increase your awareness of your energy:

Work with a partner. Stand facing your partner and center yourself. Allow your breath to become slow and deep. Inhale slowly through your nose and exhale slowly, again through your nose. Imagine as you exhale that your exhalation is flowing through your palms. Imagine the flow of breath entering through your nose and leaving through your palms. Concentrate on this for several minutes. Notice any sensations you feel in your hands. Now extend your arms slightly so your palms are close to your partner's palms but not touching. Tune into your partner's energy. Notice any sensations between your palms. As you become aware of the energy flowing between you and your partner, begin to separate. Move slowly apart, keeping your attention on your palms and on the energy flowing from you and your partner. See how far apart you can move while still keeping the energy flowing between you.

◆　◆　◆　◆　◆

The following exercise is in the form of an energy circle. You need at least two other people to stand or sit with you in a circle holding hands.

It is recommended that you each sing, hum, or chant during the following procedure:

While standing or sitting, hold your right palm down (for sending energy) and your left palm up (for receiving energy). Close your eyes and synchronize your breathing.

Visualize the circle surrounded by healing, protective energy. See the energy as a pool of liquid light at your feet. As you inhale, draw light up through the soles of your feet. Feel it move slowly throughout your body. Pull it up through your legs and into your hips. Let it move slowly along your spine. Feel it move into your shoulders and neck, down your arms and into your hands, and back up your shoulders and your neck again. Draw the energy into your head and imagine it flowing out the top of your head, spilling over and around you.

This is the energy of the universe, the energy of life. It is this energy you are connecting with, the energy you will send around the circle. Draw this energy into your body now by pulling it or by simply letting it flow into your left hand, flow throughout your body, and then out your right hand to the person on your right. Merge with the swirling, circling energy. Feel the energy.

You can end this exercise after 15 minutes by dropping your hands and opening your eyes. You may also make one of the following affirmations:

"May the energy we shared here be with us while we are apart" or "The circle is open but not broken."

◆　◆　◆　◆　◆

Other energy circle exercises are:

1. Have each person make a wish. Let everyone meditate on it, sending energy to the wisher and visualizing the wish being fulfilled.

2. Cover the nape of the neck of the person to your right and focus on the white light protection image.

3. Let everyone meditate on something of importance to the group, and direct energy toward it.

CHAPTER 5

DEVELOPING YOUR PSYCHIC AWARENESS

IN ORDER TO develop your psychic abilities, you must establish harmony within your own psyche. Many aspects of your personality and behavior probably could be improved. It is absolutely necessary first to establish a basic balance within yourself.

The energy exercises in the previous chapter will help put you on firm ground in this goal. I offer the following recommendations to facilitate your psychic foundation:

1. Accept yourself for who you are and take an inventory of your own needs.

2. Do not allow negative influences to affect you.

3. Trust in yourself and keep your motives pure.

4. Recognize that certain things and situations are outside your control and that you cannot change them.

5. Initiate changes that you can control and that result in your spiritual growth.

6. Take care of your body.

7. Do not allow any person or institution to victimize you.

8. Establish balance in every aspect of your life.

DEVELOPING YOUR ABILITY TO VISUALIZE

Many of the exercises I have already presented require some form of visualization. Television has most definitely dulled our ability to create images in our mind. This section will help nurture your natural ability to visualize.

Concentration is the first step in improving your ability to visualize. Practice these exercises when your mind is free of outside distractions. Imagination always precedes visualization.

The following exercise will help you develop your visualization skills:

Relax and think of a situation in your life that you would like to change. It must be something within your power, but something you have procrastinated about dealing with. Visualize a solution to your problem and focus on this image.

Use your psychic energy to create minute details of this plan of action. Concentrate on the actions of others in your plan. Hold this picture in your mind for as long as you can. Soon your Higher Self will assist you in this endeavor.

Feel yourself right in the middle of this plan, directing it and reaping its rewards. Keep the plan simple but direct, and execute it forcefully.

◆　◆　◆　◆　◆

These two visualization exercises will open the channels to your psychic abilities:

Relax and imagine yourself on a deserted beach at noon. See yourself writing your name in the sand and watching the waves wash it away. Smell the salt air and listen to the sound of the waves against the rocks as you walk up the shoreline. Feel the peacefulness and listen to the sound of the seagulls as they look for food.

Move to an inlet of a small lake and stand by a shallow pool of water.

Look at your reflection in this pool and see the many facets of your soul. Observe that you can be loving, jealous, angry, creative, happy, weak, and strong.

Keep looking at yourself and pinpoint the problems that can be corrected. See yourself changing and merging with the happy and strong you. See images of the dysfunctional you as you splash the water. Watch as these images disappear.

As the water clears, lean over and see yourself empowered and in complete control of your life. Watch as the pool grows wider and deeper. See how clear and clean it is. Dive into the pool and merge with your Higher Self, which is represented by the water. Finally, rise up out of the water, open your eyes, and stretch.

◆ ◆ ◆ ◆ ◆

The second exercise is this:

Relax and protect yourself. Imagine you have come upon a beautiful natural spring. You dip into that water and find it warm and inviting. The water is not deep, only up to your shoulders if you are sitting. And you do sit and relax in the warm water. The water begins to bubble and swirl around you. Swirling and whirling, the water churns over you and around you. And you feel your muscles relaxing, become more and more relaxed. The water is swirling and circling and you are letting go, letting go of tension and pain. The water is washing away all that anxiety, all that fear. And the warmth and movement of the water is soothing and relaxing you. You are releasing all that tension. Let the swirling waters soothe and heal you. When you are ready, swim up and back to your usual waking reality. And you will return relaxed, calm, and centered.

◆ ◆ ◆ ◆ ◆

MONITORING

This technique involves keeping track of your feelings and reactions to events in your life. Here is a simple exercise that will improve your psychic powers:

Note your reactions, your thoughts and feelings, to the events of the day.

Jot them down in a journal, noting the time of day these events occurred. All you need is a few words to describe your reactions.

Relax and ask your Higher Self for additional thoughts and feelings about each event. Add these to your journal. During the day review what you have written. At the end of the day, examine the entire day's recording and look for patterns and insights. This will improve your awareness of the inner you–the seat of your psychic power.

◆ ◆ ◆ ◆ ◆

This technique can also be utilized with dreams. Record your dreams and look for patterns.

The hardest thing about psychic development for most people is finding time to practice exercises. But they work, and you'll benefit from them.

BUILDING BLOCKS OF PSYCHIC DEVELOPMENT

1. *Cooperation.* This principle is based on giving and receiving in equal amounts. Since you will be working with others, this is a most important building block. It results in shared energy as well as shared experiences.

Questions to consider

A. What do you want from this relationship?

B. What changes are you willing to make?

C. How difficult is it to be the real you?

D. Are you giving enough or too much?

E. How hard is it for you to share?

2. *Discipline.* You must maintain self-control and stick to your training exercises to develop psychically. Without this self-discipline you will become out of balance and your psychic talents will suffer.

Questions to consider

A. Why do you fail?

B. Do you have difficulty planning a goal?

C. Have you sabotaged your efforts in the past?

D. Have you built a solid base for yourself?

3. *Balance.* This is a state of equilibrium, of inner and outer harmony. You must be centered to be in balance. Spiritual balance is natural.

Questions to consider

A. Does your imbalance affect others? How?

B. What do you need to do to establish balance?

C. Are you willing to make changes?

D. What obstacles currently exist in your life that contribute to this lack of balance?

4. *Vision.* This building block is a natural ability to visualize, prepare for the future, and imagine.

Questions to consider

A. Can you identify your karmic obligations and relationships?

B. Do you listen to and follow your inner voice?

C. Do you ignore opportunities to grow and tune in to others?

5. *Control.* This principle deals with regulation and taking charge of your life. When you are in control, your mind removes obstacles and your body is rejuvenated.

Questions to consider

A. Are you ready to take control of your life?

B. Can you move beyond your limitations?

C. Is there anything or anyone you fear?

6. *Release.* To release is to set free from confinement and restraint. When you liberate yourself from worry, grief, pain, and obligations, you are releasing yourself.

Questions to consider

A. Do you know what is holding you back?

B. Do you have confidence in your ability to obtain this release?

C. Can you confront negativity?

7. *Wisdom*. When you exhibit sound judgment and can differentiate between right and wrong, you are showing wisdom. It is not enough to acquire knowledge. You must put it to practical use. Wisdom is based on experience as well as knowledge.

Questions to consider

A. What mistakes have you repeated?

B. Do you consider all options when making decisions?

C. What have you learned from life?

8. *Creativity*. Being creative involves producing something from your imagination and thoughts. It is a way of transforming ideas into reality.

Questions to consider

A. What creative talents do you have?

B. What ideas would you like to see become a reality?

C. What has prevented you from expressing your talents?

9. *Individuality*. The sum total of your personality traits and other characteristics makes you unique among others and represents your individuality.

Questions to consider

A. Are you afraid of doing something different?

B. What is special about yourself?

C. Do you have a unique trait that you have been too inhibited to express?

10. Power. The energy and force to act on your convictions are your power. That is not something to be feared, unless you misuse it.

Questions to consider

A. Have you given up any of your power?

B. How can you better express your power?

C. Can you sense the inner strength you possess?

11. *Success.* When you attain goals by achievement and recognition you have exhibited success.

Questions to consider

A. What do you desire in order to be considered successful?

B. Are you prepared to make sacrifices to attain goals?

C. Who has helped and hindered your previous attempts at success?

Here are some exercises designed to help you remove fears and free up your psychic energy:

Relax and protect yourself. Find yourself at the foot of a mountain. Begin a gradual ascent now. And as you wind your way slowly along that mountain path, become aware of a heaviness, a tiredness, a sense of anger, futility, and pain. Your climb is slower and you feel those burdens you are carrying, burdens you had not even realized you asked for, but that you are carrying nevertheless. And the sun grows hotter as it climbs higher in the sky. And you travel on. Soon you come to rest by a small crevice in the rocks, and then suddenly a stream appears. The stream widens, water rushing down the rocks. You shed your clothes and stand beneath the waterfall. Feel the clear, cool water pouring down all over you. Let the gentle stream of water wash away all your fears, all your sorrows, all your anxieties.

Now, stepping out from under the waterfall, you rest for a while, letting yourself dry off in the sun. Let the sunlight stream down upon you and fill every cell and tissue until you feel light and refreshed and renewed. When you are ready, you can return to your usual awareness—relaxed, refreshed, and filled with energy.

Light some white candles, sit quietly, and allow yourself to relax fully. Now reflect on those fears or habits that you would like to release. Write each fear, habit, or negative feeling or experience on a separate piece of paper.

Take the pieces of paper one at a time and read them aloud. Then burn each one, saying, "As this paper burns, my fear is destroyed." You may want to see the negative energy transformed into positive energy. As you burn each paper, you may say, "This fire is transforming my worry into careful attention."

When you have finished burning all the papers, sit quietly and reflect on what you have said and done. Feel yourself released from fears and negative energy and filled with love and joy.

Relax and protect yourself. Travel easily to a safe mental space. Here in this space you can re-create your day, a day that has been difficult for you. Conjure up each thought, each act, each word you regret. See them all very clearly.

Now take the images one at a time and watch as they grow smaller, smaller, and smaller. Help the images grow smaller. They are dissolving, growing smaller and fainter until they no longer exist. The image no longer has the power to hurt or disturb you in any way. It is dissolved, washed away, completely erased.

And now conjure up each word, each act, each thought you enjoyed, that you consider important, anything you feel positive about. Conjure up each happy thought, fleeting smile, pleasant experience. And let these images grow. Let them become larger and larger. Let them spill over into your consciousness. You are bathed in the joy of the remembered experiences.

CHAPTER 6

BASIC TECHNIQUES OF PSYCHIC DEVELOPMENT

THE FIRST TECHNIQUE we will discuss is contacting the Higher Self. The Higher Self is the voice of the soul and is its ultimate source of wisdom and psychic energy. By accessing your Higher Self you have awareness and knowledge not available to you during your routine waking activities. Guided meditation, hypnosis, and dreams are the main paths to your Higher Self.

The Higher Self is the perfect part of your soul. It is a remnant of the energy from which everyone originated. When you complete your karmic cycle, your soul will merge with your Higher Self and you will then ascend to the higher planes of the infinite universe.

The best way to contact your Higher Self is to practice centering and clearing exercises, and also to practice different types of visualization techniques.

The next exercise is a self-hypnotic script I use with my patients to train them to contact the Higher Self. As with all such scripts, this works best if you make a tape.

CONTACTING THE HIGHER SELF

"Listen very carefully. I want you to imagine a bright white light coming down from above and entering the top of your head and filling your entire body. See it, feel it, and it becomes reality. Now imagine an aura of pure white light emanating from your heart region. Again imagine it surrounding your entire body and protecting you. See it, feel it, and it becomes reality. Now only your masters and guides and the highly evolved loving entities who mean you well will be able to influence you during this or any other hypnotic session. You are totally protected by this aura of pure white light.

"In a few moments I am going to count from one to 20. As I do so, you will feel yourself rising up to the Higher Self, where you will be able to receive information from your masters and guides. You will also be able to access your psychic energy. *1,* rising up. *2, 3, 4,* rising higher. *5, 6, 7,* letting information flow. *8, 9, 10,* you are halfway there. *11, 12, 13,* feel yourself rising even higher. *14, 15, 16,* almost there. *17, 18, 19,* practically there. *20,* you are there. Take a moment and orient yourself to the Higher Self."

(Play New Age music for one minute.)

"You may now ask yourself questions about past, present, or future issues. Or, you may contact any of your guides or departed loved ones. You may explore your relationship with any person. Remember, your Higher Self is all-knowledgeable and has access to your akashic records. These records are charts, so to speak, of your entire karmic cycle, including past and future lifetimes.

"Now slowly and carefully state your desire for information or experience and let your Higher Self work for you."

(Play New Age music for eight minutes.)

"You have done very well. Now I want you to open up further the channels of communication by removing any obstacles and allowing yourself to receive information and experiences that will directly apply to and help better your present lifetime. Allow yourself to receive more advanced and more specific information from your Higher Self and your masters and guides to raise your frequency and improve your karmic subcycle. This is a branch of your overall karmic cycle dealing only with lessons necessary for this lifetime. Also allow yourself to master your psychic powers and grow spiritually at the same time. Do this now."

(Play New Age music for eight minutes.)

"All right, now. Sleep now and rest. You did very well. Listen very carefully. I'm going to count forwards now from one to five. When I reach five, you will be back in the present. You will be able to remember everything you experienced and re-experienced, you'll feel very relaxed and refreshed, and you'll be able to do whatever you have planned for the rest of the day or evening. You'll feel very positive about what you've just experienced and very motivated about your confidence and ability to play this tape again to experience your Higher Self. All right, now. *1,* very very deep; *2,* you're getting a little bit lighter; *3,* you're getting much much lighter; *4,* very very light; *5,* awaken. Wide awake and refreshed."

◆　◆　◆　◆　◆

The Higher Self is continually communicating with us. We can accept or reject this input. The purpose of psychic development is to open yourself up to this communication.

There are only two kinds of psychic phenomena: the spontaneous and the controlled. In times of extreme danger or emotional excitement, very strange things can happen in the human mind, as everyone knows from experience. These are the spontaneous phenomena, which may happen only a few times during an entire lifetime. But the controlled phenomena can be produced at will anywhere and anytime under the right conditions and motivation. When you access your Higher Self, you control your psychic abilities.

INTUITION

We are born with intuition. The sense of direct knowing without the use of our conscious reasoning processes comprises intuition. It is a basic psychic talent.

Most people distrust their instincts and reject anything that relates to intuition. It is the rational left brain that wins the battle and buries our psychic powers. Your intuition is simply your Higher Self overriding the conscious mind and informing you of something you need to know.

The first positive step you need to take is to accept that your intuition is a component of your psychic abilities. Practice the energy exercises in Chapter 2 to develop your ability to receive information from your Higher Self.

One of the most difficult things to do is to change. It's easy to repeat old habits and ignore your intuition. Here is a list of things you can do to better yourself, initiate change, and expand your awareness to your intuition:

1. Take action
2. Love yourself.
3. Have faith.
4. Forgive.
5. Start again.
6. Meditate.
7. Be free.
8. Let go.
9. Have no regrets.
10. Be receptive to the world.
11. Change.
12. Give back.

Intuition comes in two main forms. They are antecedent intuition and intuition without antecedent.

ANTECEDENT INTUITION

This kind of intuition requires the mind to have been prepared with certain information to arrive at some conclusion. Most of our ordinary problem solving is completed with this type of intuition. Your subconscious processes myriad information, finds the correct answer to a problem, and releases that answer in the form of an insight.

People often acquire these remarkable insights while dreaming. Many a scientific breakthrough was initiated by a researcher waking up with a brilliant idea and testing it immediately.

INTUITION WITHOUT ANTECEDENT

When you get a sudden inspiration that appears "out of the blue," you have experienced intuition without antecedent. You just appear to know something, and it is not difficult to find a practical use for this information. It often is preceded by an emergency or crisis. This form is uncontrolled and can be very upsetting, since you are never prepared to receive this information. This latter category is generally labeled "psychic," because it is characterized by "just knowing."

Both types of intuition function as satellite dishes continually scanning the skies for signals. Only when you open yourself up to receive these signals will intuition come to the surface.

THE PHILOSOPHER'S STONE

One of the most esoteric practices deals with what is known as the Philosopher's Stone. Medieval alchemists thought that this stone could turn base metals into gold.

The purpose of a Philosopher's Stone nowadays is not to transform metals but to develop psychic powers. A rock represents strength. It comes from nature. Once it is prepared, it becomes a focal point for your psychic energy.

The Philosopher's Stone represents wisdom, protection, purpose, and strength. It is a starting point for communication with your Higher Self. It can facilitate your spiritual growth and shorten your karmic cycle.

The first step in selecting your stone is to visualize what you think it should look like. Look for this stone in your community. It might be in your backyard, on the beach, in the mountains, or it might be a crystal you purchase in a store. Take your time and let the vibrations you feel while holding this stone, along with your own natural intuition, help you select it.

Find a special place in your home for your stone. Some people keep their Philosopher's Stone in a special box. It can be decorative and placed in the living room. Ideally, your stone should be placed on a wooden stand and covered with a white cloth.

Once you have selected your stone, it must be prepared for use. Wash it in tepid water. You can use a soft washcloth and dishwashing liquid if you choose.

Rinse the stone in tepid water and immediately place it on a white towel. Once it has dried, wrap it in the white cloth you will use to cover it when it is placed on its wooden stand.

Dust your stone daily, as dust interferes with psychic energy. Repeat the preparation procedure annually on your stone's anniversary date.

The psychic energy in your Philosopher's Stone will be rejuvenated by this annual procedure.

The following exercise will boost your psychic power and increase your confidence that your level of psychic development will continue to grow.

Relax and play metaphysical music. Bathe and wear loose clothes. Make sure you are facing east.

Place your wrapped-up stone on a purple cloth. Place four white candles around it, facing north, south, east, and west of your stone. Light the candles. Place a bowl of water and a white hand towel to the left of your stone.

Next, place your left hand in the bowl of water. Remove your hand and shake the water over your stone, still wrapped in its cloth, three times.

Blow out the candles in the following order: north, south, east, and west of the stone. Lift the wrapped-up stone and say, "I direct the focus of my Higher Self to the center of the stone. I seek the psychic energy contained within this stone."

Remove the stone from its cloth wrapper and place it directly on the purple cloth in the center of the blown-out candles.

Place both hands in the bowl of water and say, "As my hands are cleansed, my subconscious requests the assistance of my Higher Self."

Dry your hands on the white hand towel and relight the candles in the following order: north, south, east, and west.

Stretch your arms over the stone with your palms facing downward. Now state: "I now activate the psychic energy within the stone."

You may sense energy coming from the stone and entering your hands and arms. You are perfectly safe. Visualize yourself in the center of the stone, bathing in its psychic energy.

You are now the Philosopher. The stone is merely a symbol and extra source of psychic energy. You have now tapped into the power of the stone and your very soul is being filled with wisdom and psychic energy.

Stand up and face the stone. Blow out each candle in the following order: north, south, east, and west. State the following: "I now possess psychic strength and power. I no longer have doubts or fears."

Now affirm, "I am the Philosopher. I am endowed with wisdom and psychic energy. This is my stone, which I will protect. My psychic powers will always be enhanced when I use this stone, but I am not dependent solely on this stone for my psychic abilities."

◆ ◆ ◆ ◆ ◆

LIFE ENERGY

The human body has life energy that flows throughout the physical body. This is often considered the universal energy (the Higher Self or perfect component of the soul's energy). When you develop your psychic abilities, your subconscious tunes in to this energy and uses it to direct its actions.

It is important that you remove negativity and stagnation from your life energy. To get the most out of the next exercise, I suggest the following:

1. Sit in an uncluttered room.

2. Remove all jewelry. Dress loosely and lightly.

3. Remove your slippers or shoes. Wear socks or keep your feet bare.

4. Play soothing background music, preferably New Age music.

The following exercise will help you get in touch with your life energy and will help you increase your psychic awareness:

Sit in a comfortable chair and relax. Close your eyes and visualize yourself entering the very depths of your soul.

Guide your soul in the direction of a white light located in the center of your being. You will feel a pull of energy. Merge with this energy.

Sense vibrations, sounds, and colors. Observe them but do not analyze them. Refrain from becoming emotional. Pay particular attention to sensations in your neck and on your face. Feel rejuvenated.

Visualize gold rays of light in the form of threads spinning around your body. These threads are lifting you up and freeing your soul from the inhibitions of the physical body and the conscious mind.

Perceive things differently now. You have just increased your spiritual vision. You can hear and feel things better now.

Move your arms and legs to allow this charged life energy to travel throughout your physical body. Feel the freedom of your psychic energy and your soul. Enjoy these sensations and encourage these feelings.

Visualize white light entering and surrounding your entire body. This white light is filled with your life energy, now psychically charged.

Step back into your physical body as you imagine the golden threads gently lowering your very essence back to your physical awareness. Slowly stretch your body, take three deep breaths, and open your eyes.

◆　◆　◆　◆　◆

To summarize the purpose of this chapter: consider your own spiritual and psychic source. Your Higher Self controls the flow of your psychic gifts. You must discipline yourself, cleanse yourself of emotional baggage and negativity, and request this psychic energy from your Higher Self.

The white light is always the key to psychic development. It not only represents protection and acts as a reference point, it is your Higher Self. You must merge with it to develop psychically.

Your conscious mind, or defense mechanisms, represents the only real obstacle to your spiritual growth and psychic development. You can use any number of methods to circumvent these obstacles. In this book I present many techniques to do this.

Never be afraid to ask your Higher Self for information or guidance. If you are not ready for such wisdom, your Higher Self will simply refrain from giving it to you. You will never be punished or harmed in any way for making this request. This is part of your psychic empowerment.

CHAPTER 7

ADVANCED TECHNIQUES OF PSYCHIC DEVELOPMENT

CLAIRVOYANCE

The psychic ability to "see" what cannot be detected by our five senses is known as clairvoyance. The following exercise will assist you in developing this ability:

Relax, breathe deeply, and sit in a comfortable chair. Close your eyes and imagine a closed door right in front of you.

Visualize yourself opening the door and looking out. Do not go through the door or think about it. Just observe the other side.

Close the door in your mind, open your eyes, and touch an object close to you. Jot down what you saw but do not analyze it.

Repeat this procedure, but this time visualize yourself going through the door. Observe how you feel and what you "see." Do not attempt to think about it.

Turn around in your mind and go back through the door. Close it, open your eyes again, and touch the same object you touched before. Again jot down your observations without analyzing them.

◆ ◆ ◆ ◆ ◆

Notice how these visualizations come to you. You do not need to seek them out. The purpose of touching the object is to return your focus to the earth plane. Review the notes you take to monitor your progress. As you review them, do not be surprised if you visualize more.

Eventually you will no longer require the door or the object to touch. These are only to train and discipline your mind to facilitate your psychic development.

When you begin to work with other people, you will appreciate this training. All your psychic senses and abilities will come into play then. Your feelings, thoughts, and voice can be used to increase your intuition and expand your psychic awareness. Your voice channels the emotions, and the vibrations from the sound waves created reflect your contact with the Higher Self.

CRYSTAL BALL

The use of a crystal ball is very old and is ingrained in the public imagination, mostly due to Hollywood. The use of a crystal ball is based on a sound metaphysical principle and is an efficient method for psychic development.

Here is a simple exercise you can use with any crystal ball:

Clean the crystal ball. Have the crystal ball positioned between you and your subject. Touch the crystal ball, take your subject's hand, and again touch the crystal ball.

Relax and breathe deeply. Clear your mind and look through the crystal ball. Do not stare at it. This technique is similar to the one used in seeing auras. You are looking through the crystal ball, not at it. Auras, too, are seen indirectly, not by staring. (See Chapter 3.)

As you gaze at the crystal ball, simply observe what you see. Do not analyze the images or expect to see anything. You are projecting your psychic energy onto the crystal ball while attempting to tap into the soul energy of your subject.

Ask your subject questions. Repeat the questions to the crystal ball. Pause for a minute or so.

When you are done or the images stop forming, gently rub the crystal ball clockwise with a velvet cloth. Touch the crystal one last time and wrap it in this cloth.

◆ ◆ ◆ ◆ ◆

A crystal ball can send energy. It can also receive positive and negative energy from people and things. That is why, according to ancient doctrine, it should always be wrapped in a velvet cloth between uses.

PENDULUMS

A pendulum may be made of anything, even a rock suspended from a chain or cord. Many psychics use specially prepared crystals as the heavy object. A pendulum is an extension of your psychic energy.

When you use your pendulum, you may use either hand to hold the cord that suspends it. The pendulum should hang from the back of the index finger. The first thing you must do is calibrate the pendulum to establish reference points and accuracy.

One way to do this is to write a question on a piece of paper and touch the pendulum to the paper. Then ask, "Did I write this question?" The pendulum will either move back and forth or in a circle. This establishes a "Yes" reference point.

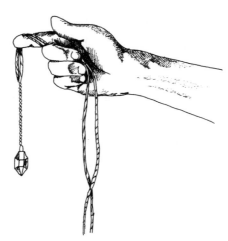

Repeat this procedure, only now write an obviously false statement on another sheet of paper. For example, a woman might state, "I am male." The movement of the pendulum in response to this is your "No" reference. It may take a few tries to establish this code. Be patient, and always use white light protection prior to using your pendulum.

To assure continued accuracy with your pendulum, the following rules are suggested:

1. Place the pendulum in a small pouch and carry it near your body.

2. Never use it to make decisions you could easily make yourself.

3. Focus only on one question at a time and clear your mind of other thoughts.

4. Do not let other people touch your pendulum or use it.

5. Do not ask the same question twice.

6. Use your pendulum when you are by yourself. The presence of other people's energy may affect the pendulum's movement.

7. If you are using the pendulum for someone else, remember to apply protection to yourself before beginning the exercises.

There are basically four ways the pendulum can move: in a counter-clockwise circle, in clockwise circle, in a line from left to right (or right to left), or back and forth in front of you. Here is a more elaborate system for using your pendulum:

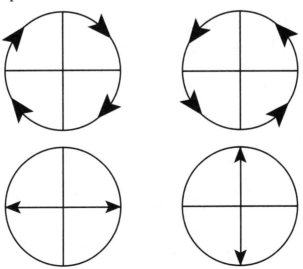

Notice how all four possible movements are presented. To expand your answers you can make each type as follows:

These four ways the pendulum can move should first be calibrated. Establish the answers that correspond to each of these types of movement. The placement of these four possible responses may be different from those illustrated here. Although pendulum movement may be slight, the arc of the swing is very definite and long.

The following exercise may be used to locate missing people, objects, or animals. You will need a personal article (dog collar, ring, etc.), photograph, drawing, or handwriting sample. A map showing where the person or animal was last seen is ideal.

> Place the item on a table and set up your pendulum. Ask where the person, item, or animal is. If you are using a map, replace it with larger-scale maps when your focus area narrows as you get affirmative responses.

> Most answers are going to be "Yes," "No," or "I don't know." Phrase your questions carefully to pinpoint the exact location you are searching for. To find a lost article in your home, draw the room where you think the misplaced item is, or draw the entire house if it can be anywhere. Repeat the procedures described above.

Another exercise that is fun and that can be used to calibrate your pendulum is to ask for the time of your birth. The following exercise will help you accomplish this simple task:

> On a piece of paper draw 12 squares and number them one through 12.

a.m.	1	2	3	4
	5	6	7	8
p.m.	9	10	11	12

HOUR CHART

Write "AM" and "PM" on the left side of this paper. This is for the exact hour of your birth. On a separate sheet of paper make a chart of 60 squares and number them 00 through 59. Number the last box 00. This 00 is in case you were born exactly on the hour. This latter chart represents the minutes of your birth. Note the following figures:

1	2	3	4	5	6	7	8	9	10
11	12	13	14	15	16	17	18	19	20
21	22	23	24	25	26	27	28	29	30
31	32	33	34	35	36	37	38	39	40
41	42	43	44	45	46	47	48	49	50
51	52	53	54	55	56	57	58	59	00

MINUTE CHART

If you are doing this for another person, touch an article of that person with the pendulum before continuing. Hold the pendulum over the AM section of the hour chart. Say the person's name. If the answer is negative, repeat this procedure over the PM section.

Continue with each number in the hour chart until you obtain a positive answer. Repeat this procedure using the minute chart.

◆　◆　◆　◆　◆

DOWSING

This ancient art of divination requires a rod made of wood, metal, or other natural material. The "Y" shape is most commonly used. Place one hand on each of the two elongations of the "Y" and use the single branch as the detector.

Hold the rod horizontally directly in front of you. Walk briskly. Gently move the rod from side to side. Relax and concentrate on whatever you are seeking–water, gold, oil, a missing object, etc.

Visualize what you are trying to find and say "water" (or whatever you are seeking) over and over as you walk.

You will know you have found what you are seeking when the rod turns and twists up and down. Sometimes it actually vibrates.

THOUGHT-FORMING

It is unethical to use this method for things that belong to others. With thought-forming, you use your psychic energy to create changes. Do not use this method to create money or to harm anyone or anything.

The easiest way to practice thought-forming is to write down on a piece of paper something you want. Relax, protect yourself, and focus on what you have written. Gaze at something in front of you and ask your Higher Self for help. Now forget about this procedure and put the paper away for 24 hours. Repeat this exercise at the same time of the day after 24, 48, and 72 hours.

Here are some ethical applications of this technique:

1. You run a business and need more customers. Visualize many people coming into your store, buying various items, and looking very satisfied with you and your enterprise.

2. Prior to a job interview, visualize yourself very poised, confident, and being offered the position. See the letter of acceptance in your hand. This can also be used for applications to colleges.

3. If you are struggling to sell your house, create an image of a "sold" sign posted on your front lawn. See yourself receiving a good price for your house in the form of an escrow check placed in your hand.

Thought-forming is commonly used unknowingly in dysfunctional ways. Women who constantly attract the same type of "Mr. Wrong" into their lives are thought-forming dysfunctionally. This exercise teaches you how to use a natural psychic gift correctly while developing your psychic awareness.

TELEPATHY

Telepathy is simply a form of thought transference whereby a person is able to communicate with another without using any of the five senses. Most people report these occurrences at least once in their lives. One example of telepathy is the mother who senses the mood of her children. Another example is the phenomenon of thinking of someone you haven't spoken to or seen in a long time and then quickly receiving a telephone call from that person.

The following is an exercise to practice with a partner whom you like and trust:

Relax. Select a time when both of you will be undisturbed. One of you will be the sender and the other the receiver.

On a separate piece of paper the sender writes words such as "vacation," "love," "food," etc. Each of these papers is folded and they are mixed up. The sender then selects one paper at random and reads the word silently.

Both sender and receiver sit facing each other, eyes closed. The sender concentrates on the selected word, creates a mental image of the word, and focuses on both the image and the word.

This process continues until the receiver gets either an image or the word itself. The receiver then shares the information with the sender.

◆　◆　◆　◆　◆

This technique requires practice, so don't expect to succeed the first time. With a little experience and psychic development this will be a routine procedure.

ESP CARDS

This exercise is a lot of fun. These cards have been used for ESP research since the early part of the century.

A set of ESP cards consists of 25 white cards with five cards each of the following five different shapes drawn in black:

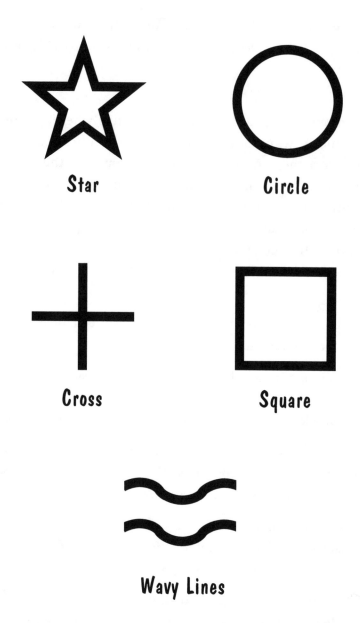

Some people substitute a triangle for the cross or star. The shapes really do not matter, as long as they are different enough from one another.

The cards should all be the same size. You can tape drawings of these figures to 25 regular playing cards.

TESTING YOURSELF WITH ESP CARDS

Have a partner sit some distance away from you with the deck. Your partner shuffles the cards, turns them over one at a time, and records your responses on a form similar to this one.

Date_____

Test subject_____ Test administered by_____

Comments:_____

TRIAL NO.	CARD DRAWN	REPLY	ACCURACY
1			In this column (labeled
2			"accuracy"), use a "+" sign
3			to indicate correct identifi-
4			cation (hit) and a "−" to
5			indicate an incorrect one
6			(miss).
7			
8			Statistically, 20% accuracy
9			or better indicates psychic
10			development. The greater
11			the accuracy, the greater
12			the level of psychic
13			development.
14			
15			
16			
17			
18			
19			
20			
21			
22			
23			
24			
25			

ESP Card Test Run

PRECOGNITION

Awareness of future events before they actually occur is a form of knowledge known as precognition. This is a main component of intuition and is unquestionably the most common of psychic experiences. In my Los Angeles hypnotherapy practice I refer to this as progression.

I have designed a simple exercise to train you to experience precognition and enhance your psychic development. The following procedure is a good introduction to this technique:

You will need to use a mental screen, such as a television set, to project future events.

Select a topic or situation that will occur in the near future and that excites you. An example would be a newspaper headline you imagine yourself reading.

Relax and then, using your mental screen, visualize your entire day during which this event will occur. Imagine yourself showering, eating breakfast, working, and so on. Carry this imagery to the end of the day.

For example, see yourself buying a newspaper on the way home from work or on an errand. Now visualize yourself sitting down and reading the headline. Jot down your results in your psychic journal. For other types of events, try to place yourself in as real a situation as you can relative to the event and where you are likely to be.

◆   ◆   ◆   ◆   ◆

Try this exercise several times. Choose more important situations as you become more proficient with this technique.

Another precognition exercise will help you develop this natural and useful psychic gift:

Relax, apply protection, and visualize a series of five doors, each with the word "future" printed on it in large, bold letters. These doors are numbered 1 through 5.

Think of a situation or upcoming event you would like to explore. Gather the actual factors you currently have available on this circumstance and review them in your mind.

Now open the door labeled "Future 1" and perceive how this situation will unfold. Observe as many details as you can. Refrain from becoming emotionally involved with this option.

Repeat this procedure for the doors labeled "Future 2," "Future 3," "Future 4," and "Future 5."

Choose the door that best meets your needs and meditate on the number of that door for two minutes.

You have just created your own reality.

◆　◆　◆　◆　◆

Precognition has many useful applications. It helps prepare you for challenges and allows you to change these events or maximize experiences. You can avoid negative circumstances in life by taking advantage of this psychic ability. Precognition also offers the opportunity to solve problems. A third advantage of precognition is that it helps you to expand your psychic awareness and enrich your life.

By using precognition you can alter the future and empower yourself. This will result in a new outlook on life–not to manipulate or control the future, but to grow spiritually and shape your destiny. The future represents probabilities, not predestined fate. Everyone has choices. By developing your psychic abilities you can expand these choices and maximize your potential.

FORECASTING

By far the most commonly requested service of a psychic is predicting, or forecasting, future events. Pure chance dictates that the average person will be correct 50 percent of the time in forecasting. When you use your psychic energy your success rate should be at least 75 percent.

I must caution you about negative information. Do not frighten people with doom-and-gloom forecasts if you are forecasting for others. The future is not fixed. It's possible to change the future by taking the appropriate action.

You can truthfully say to the person you are forecasting for, "You are under an influence that could lead to a car accident. I recommend caution in the next few days while driving." This way, you warn the person of impending danger but refrain from causing excess anxiety. Use your common sense in these matters.

In order to master the art of forecasting, you will need to become familiar with your *timeline*. Your particular and unique relationship with time is your timeline.

Here are some simple questions to help you determine your timeline:

1. Do you wake up just a few minutes before your alarm clock?

2. Are you punctual?

3. Can you lose moments of time easily?

4. Are you accurately aware of the time without looking at a watch?

The more accurate you are in your judgment of time, the easier it will be for you to fine-tune your forecasting ability.

The following exercise will assist you in finding your timeline.

Sit comfortably and close your eyes. Visualize a road that stretches out in front of you in two directions. Each road has a sign. One sign says "past" and the other, "future."

Begin by taking the "past" road. Be aware of time as you do so. Does yesterday feel very different from last year or from five years ago?

Do the same thing with the "future" road. Travel on this road as far as you like and note events occurring and the relative feeling of each block of time. Return to the present.

Decide which timeline you want to use for predictions. Most commonly, you will choose the future. Select an actual event that you want to forecast.

Relax and focus on this event as you travel on the timeline road. Look around and sense everything you can. Return to the present.

Open your eyes. Using your psychic journal, write down all thoughts, feelings, and impressions you obtained.

◆ ◆ ◆ ◆ ◆

The first few times you practice this exercise, choose a time close to the present. This way you can easily check your forecasting for accuracy.

As you develop your psychic talents, you can increase the timeline and forecast far into the future.

This technique works best with specific questions. You may ask general questions, but be prepared for a slower and more general response.

PSYCHIC RECEPTIVITY DISCOVERY EXERCISE

This exercise is designed to assist you in identifying your natural mode of psychic awareness. You may be predominantly clairaudient (hearing psychic input), clairsentient (feeling psychic information), or clairvoyant (seeing psychic data).

This exercise requires visual imagery and a relaxed state:

Relax, close your eyes, and visualize yourself in a large room with a table. On this table are three masks. Each one is different. They are labeled "seeing," "hearing," and "feeling." Take a few moments to focus on what these masks look like.

Imagine yourself moving across the room and opening a door that leads to an underground chamber. Descend the stairs until you end up in this chamber. This is where your intuition resides.

Now open another door, leading to your psychic mode room. There is one mask on a table in this room. Slowly walk up to this table and pick up the mask. It is one of the three you viewed earlier. Which psychic mode is it?

Pick up the mask and put it on. A mirror is in front of you. Walk up to the mirror and look at yourself. The mask is labeled "seeing," "hearing," or "feeling." The word is written backwards on the mask. When you look in the mirror it correctly spells out one of these psychic modes. Which is it?

Stay with this image for a few minutes. Slowly open your eyes and jot down your observations in your psychic journal.

◆　◆　◆　◆　◆

If your mask read "seeing," you are clairvoyant. Clairaudient would be your psychic mode if your mask read "hearing." Finally, you are clairsentient if you saw the word "feeling." Usually this exercise is not necessary, as most people would have noted their psychic mode much earlier in this book. You may have more than one mode represented by your natural psychic abilities, but one mode usually dominates.

THE ENERGY CROSSOVER

This exercise is meant to increase your psychic bond with another person when you are reading him or her. This procedure has many applications in psychic healing.

When practicing this exercise, select a person you like or feel comfortable with:

You and the other person each relax and close your eyes, apply protection, and sit facing one another.

Mentally send a line of energy from a point midway between yourself and this subject. This energy goes around the right side of the other person, goes around the person's back, and emerges on the left side. It then crosses over midway between the two of you, passes by your left side, goes around your back, emerges from your right side, and returns to the point of origin. A figure eight results.

Stay with this image for 20 minutes. Observe colors, pain, images, and anything else emanating from the other person. You are both sending and receiving energy at this time.

Open up your eyes and watch the other person.

End this exercise by mentally cutting the figure eight with a large pair of scissors. Open your eyes and sip some water.

◆　◆　◆　◆　◆

This technique can be used to increase creativity, remove blocks, find missing objects or people. Always sever this energy line when you are done. Do not allow this procedure to drain you of energy unnecessarily, especially when you are unprotected.

AUTOMATIC WRITING

When information is obtained from the subconscious by spontaneous or involuntary writing, this is called automatic writing. Initial efforts usually result in illegible and disorganized scribbling impossible to understand.

As you develop your psychic awareness, this skill sharpens and the automatic writing you produce will bear readable words, phrases, and sentences. Sometimes this produces figures or symbols.

Some psychics have used automatic writing techniques to find missing persons and lost articles. Automatic writing gives direct access to the subconscious, without any need to interpret or feel a vibration. It results in written communication that anyone can read and understand.

The following exercises will give you a good introduction to this fascinating technique:

Relax, apply protection, and breathe deeply for a few moments.

At the top of a sheet of paper write a question you want answered or a problem you want solved.

Meditate on this question and place a pen and a tablet of writing paper in your normal writing hand.

Ask your Higher Self for assistance and block out all thoughts and feelings related to your question or anything else. It is desirable to have soothing metaphysical music playing in the background during this exercise.

Slowly, draw a small circle and keep moving your hand in a clockwise direction, as you focus on accessing your psychic energy.

Your hand should shortly begin to write on its own. Do not open up your eyes or try to monitor your writing. Let the writing occur naturally.

◆　◆　◆　◆　◆

This technique requires patience and it may take several attempts to produce the desired results.

A second exercise includes self-hypnosis. Begin the usual way and place yourself or someone else in a trance in the manner you are most comfortable with. Then dissociate the writing hand from the rest of the body. You can use the following script:

"Your hand will get numb and cold; it is losing all feeling, all sensation, and all movement. You do not feel your hand as I rub it. It is getting very numb, and it no longer feels attached to your wrist. Now, as you raise your arm, it will feel as if the hand is no longer attached to the arm. You no longer have any control over your hand. However, your hand can remember everything about you. If you cannot remember something in particular about yourself, your hand will be able to remember it and will write out the answer. If it is too painful for you to face or talk about, your hand will write it. Your hand will write the correct answer without your controlling it. Your subconscious will now answer the question I asked."

After your writing is completed, end the trance in the usual way. The last thing you suggest to the subconscious is, "You will easily recognize what you have written."

◆　◆　◆　◆　◆

PSYCHOKINESIS

The ability of the mind to influence objects, processes, and events without the aid of instruments or physical energy is called psychokinesis, or PK. PK mostly occurs as a spontaneous, goal-driven phenomenon.
PK is known to occur in four stages. These are:

1. *Alert Stage.* This is a readiness stage, characterized by perceiving a desired result, expecting success, and having a clear objective. PK powers are increased by a positive mental attitude during this stage.

2. *Centering Stage.* PK energies are now created either spontaneously or by focused concentration. They are guided mentally into an appropriate image or energy.

3. *Focus Stage.* PK energies are now directed at a specific target. You must maintain continued focused concentration for this stage to be effective.

4. *Releasing Stage.* Now the focused energies are released. Direct commands can now bring about movement, stillness, bending, repair of tissue, or other healing effects.

PSYCHOKINESIS EXERCISES

Relax, apply protection, and breathe deeply.

Mentally envision a coin you are about to flip landing on "heads." Stay with this thought for three minutes.

Flip the coin and continue focusing your psychic energy on it.

Continue bombarding the coin with your energy and with verbal commands to land on "heads."

Continue until the coin comes to rest.

◆　◆　◆　◆　◆

Repeat the above procedure with dice, moving a pendulum, a compass, a stationary light object, such as a pencil or bottle cap. This technique requires a lot of practice and mastery of your psychic energy to be performed successfully. This is truly an advanced technique of psychic development.

CHAPTER 8

COLOR AND PSYCHIC DEVELOPMENT

CHAPTER 3 DISCUSSED the psychic significance of color in relation to auras. Color exerts an effect on mood, behavior, and attitude. Color is part of nature and cannot be avoided. Think of the blue skies, green grass, brown tree trunks, and multi-colored flowers.

The change of seasons causes vast color changes. Not only humans respond to these changes. Color is also important to animals, especially with the change of seasons. Many animals change color to blend in with their environment. Mating and hunting depend on these color changes.

The impact of color–from the beauty of nature to the food we eat and the clothes we wear–cannot be overestimated. Activities can be enhanced or retarded by color.

At one end of the color spectrum are blue, indigo, and violet. These have a relaxing effect and are good background colors for a room. Orange, red, and yellow are at the other end of the color spectrum. These are good for accentuating a room.

Green adds strength and stability because it is in the middle of the color spectrum. Everyone responds differently to color. That is why green is not the most popular color. One might expect it would be, since it is in the middle of the color spectrum. Some realtors say that the best color in a house for sale is yellow. Yellow, remember, is at one end of the color spectrum.

Color has important psychic effects. It can stimulate the subconscious and facilitate contact with the Higher Self. This is very important in meditation and hypnosis. Too much or too little color may exert an unhealthful influence on psychic balance. White light protection is an example of the positive use of color to maintain a balance in psychic energy.

Candles are often used in psychic development exercises. The flame of a lit candle represents energy, life, and light. Mood can be affected quickly by burning certain color candles, and the energy vibration from a lit candle can be quite exhilarating and healing (see Chapter 9).

The following chart shows the positive and negative effects of the seven colors of the rainbow:

COLOR	POSITIVE EFFECT	NEGATIVE EFFECT
VIOLET	INNER WISDOM	IGNORANCE
INDIGO	BALANCE	CHAOS
BLUE	FREEDOM	PROCRASTINATION
GREEN	DISCIPLINE	SELF-RESTRICTION
YELLOW	SELF-EXPRESSION	CONCEIT
ORANGE	COOPERATION	SELFISHNESS
RED	INDIVIDUALITY	LOSS OF IDENTITY

COLOR AND FOOD

Food color has an effect on you, and you are what you eat. If you list everything you eat on a typical day, you will better appreciate the importance of color and behavior.

Begin with a typical American breakfast. Coffee provides the stimulus for creativity and gives substance to the emotions. Orange juice encourages cooperation due to its color. Yellow scrambled eggs lend the ability to be expressive. The yellow color also stimulates the emotional level.

Consider the psychic or esoteric effects of foods. Foods rich in orange, yellow, and red help increase physical, mental, and psychic energy. These effects are not the same for everyone.

The following exercise will help you to place your regular foods into color groups. Fill in these blanks and meditate on this list when it is complete:

COLOR	FOODS IN YOUR DAILY DIET	SAMPLE FOODS
VIOLET		eggplant, blackberries
BLUE		grapes, blueberries
GREEN		lettuce, beans
YELLOW		bananas, lemons
ORANGE		oranges, carrots
RED		beets, tomatoes

YOUR PSYCHIC COLORS

Which of the seven rainbow colors is best for you psychically? There is no pat answer, but fortunately an exercise can help determine this.

Wear loose white clothes. Do not wear jewelry or anything that has color. Prepare seven pieces of fabric, one for each of the seven rainbow colors. Any material is acceptable, but silk is the best.

Do this exercise with another person. For simplicity, let's refer to the person conducting this exercise as the teacher. Refer to the person being tested as the subject.

The subject should stand on a white object (such as a rug or a pillowcase), feet apart and eyes closed. The subject's arms should be positioned away from the body and pointed downward, hands stretched open.

The teacher should be dressed in white with no jewelry and should stand, eyes closed, six feet (180 cm) from the subject. The teacher takes three deep breaths and visualizes a white light around both their bodies.

The subject stretches out the left hand and the teacher places one of the colored pieces of fabric in this hand. The teacher, using the right hand, now presses on the subject's left upper arm and asks the subject to resist. This is done three times. The results are noted in a journal.

The teacher takes the same cloth and places it in the subject's right hand and the test is repeated three times. Again the results are noted in a journal.

After a short rest break, this test is repeated with each of the remaining six cloths.

◆　◆　◆　◆　◆

The results are then noted. The subject's resistance to each color is noted as strong, weak, nonexistent, or normal. A weak response to the color green, for example, indicates the subject lacks discipline. This is only at the time of the test, and various healing procedures could be employed to correct this situation (see Chapter 9).

One simple and immediate solution in the above example would be for the subject to meditate with green candles, wear more green, and eat foods that are green in color.

Any medical problems should be referred to a physician, because these procedures do not replace medical treatment. After a week to 10 days of the subject adding more of the deficient color, run these tests again and note any differences. You may notice significant improvement in that short a time.

Pay special attention to the colors of your bed sheets and your car. You spend a lot of time there and these colors will be important to your psychic energy. You can neutralize the effect of car colors by wearing certain other colors. Replace bed sheets if the colors are wrong for your energy.

USING COLOR TO REMOVE NEGATIVITY

Chapter 4 describes several exercises to establish spiritual protection. In all cases they involve surrounding your body with a white light. This section will use various colors to neutralize negativity that may be affecting you.

Sources of negativity may be relationships, employers, employees, institutions, neighbors, and even strangers. These can all drain energy. You must deal with this negativity or it will interfere with your subconscious ability to tap into your Higher Self. Without this connection, your psychic development will be significantly limited.

For this exercise wear loose fitting clothes and no jewelry:

Place seven white candles on a table that contains a pen, a sheet of paper, and a vase full of freshly cut flowers of several different colors. The flowers symbolize positiveness and life. Center the vase on the table and place a comfortable chair near the table. Now, place two glasses of water on the table, one each to the left and right of the vase.

Relax yourself, take a deep breath and light the first candle. Stare into the flame of this candle and ask your Higher Self to assist you in balancing your individuality.

Sit down at the table and write all the characteristics of your individuality that need improvement or are no longer useful. Fold the paper in half and meditate on it for one minute. Now place the paper in the flame and say, "I now remove this negativity from my soul as the flame consumes this paper."

Light the second white candle and repeat the procedure, this time regarding your relationships.

Light the third candle and repeat the procedure, this time regarding your creative energy.

Light the fourth candle and repeat the procedure, this time regarding your self-discipline.

Light the fifth candle and repeat the procedure, this time regarding your freedom.

Light the sixth candle and repeat the procedure, this time regarding your harmony on all levels of consciousness.

If you are curious about the reason your soul chose this current lifetime, repeat the procedure and light the seventh candle, this time regarding your karmic purpose.

Wait seven minutes after the last exercise before approaching these seven candles one more time and asking your Higher Self to grant these requests. Visualize each one of these goals being accomplished.

Now drink from the glass of water on your left and then the one on your right. As you drink from each glass say, "As I drink this water I am purifying and cleansing my soul."

◆　◆　◆　◆　◆

The next exercise will assist you in using color to balance your psychic energy and establish harmony between your body, mind, and spirit. Each color has its own vibratory rate and interacts with your aura. It is critical that you learn to interpret this effect and use this knowledge to reverse or balance out negativity for yourself and others.

The following chart represents specific issues you may want to work on with each of these seven colored candles:

COLOR	GOALS TO WORK ON
Purple	philosophy
	wisdom
	inspiration
	intellect
Indigo	service
	karmic purpose
	balance
	consciousness
Blue	versatility
	freedom
	resources
	needs
Green	foundations
	effort
	discipline
	organization
Yellow	expression
	talents
	enthusiasm
	creativity
Orange	relationships
	concern for others
	cooperation
	consideration
Red	needs
	desires
	individuality
	strength

Too much or too little of certain colors can cause irritability, sleeping problems, and other difficulties. Part of your karmic purpose is to prevent these forms of victimization and to empower yourself at every level of awareness.

Use the following exercise to test items in your home. Anything with color has a potential influence on you. You might want to check sheets, socks, towels, pants, blouses, scarves, and handkerchiefs.

Before working on this exercise, practice the previous procedure at least three times. You were able to determine the influence of the seven colors of the rainbow on someone else. Now switch roles with your partner so you can determine these effects on yourself.

The purpose of this exercise is to feel the energy level of each of these seven colors—violet, indigo, blue, green, yellow, orange, and red. You will need seven candles, one for each of these colors. With the results of the previous exercise, you can now alter your focus to attain balance.

For example, if you have too little green in your life, spend more time with the green-candle procedure. If you have too much of the effect of a particular color at this time, try to tone down your use of it.

Interpretation is very important in this exercise. A lighter shade of a certain color means a decrease in the vibratory level of that hue. An increase in this vibratory level is observed with darker shades. Knowing these effects, you can adjust each color and obtain a true energy balance.

Red is a good color to use as an example. If you feel insecure, you are likely to sense a paler red color. You would experience a darker tone of red if you are too aggressive.

You will also need an extra white candle. The best way to do this exercise is immediately after three practice sessions with the previous procedure. At the end of that technique I instructed you to burn white candles for seven minutes.

The arrangements are as follows:

Light your original seven white candles.

Place the extra white candle to the left of this group and light it. It should be within arm's reach of you. I will refer to this candle now as the catalyst.

Before you are seven colored candles. They represent the seven colors of the rainbow: purple, indigo, blue, green, yellow, orange, and red.

Bring the catalyst candle in front of you and meditate on it for one minute, asking your Higher Self for assistance in balancing your psychic energy.

Return this candle to its original position to the left of the seven white candles.

Remove the red candle and use the catalyst candle to light it. Place the catalyst candle to the left of this lit red candle.

Take one of the seven original white candles and place it to the right of the red candle.

Balancing occurs now. The left catalyst candle represents the source of your spiritual energy and the hidden parts of your awareness. The right represents the manifestation of your psychic energy through the vibration of the color. The center represents the balance of these two energies.

Now focus your attention on the red candle, spreading your arms out in the direction of the left and right candles. Ask your Higher Self to balance your true individuality.

Become aware of any deficient or excessive red energy. You will feel the energy vibration from the red candle. Concentrate on your natural response to your individuality.

Spend a few minutes on this meditation and ask your Higher Self for guidance in evaluating how much or little red should be in your life at this time.

Be aware of the tendency of your body to lean to the left or right while you are meditating. Open your psychic energy to feel the flow of individuality emanating from the red candle.

Use your hand to center your body between the two candles and to remain directly in front of the catalyst candle. Continue shifting your position until you feel a perfect psychic balance of this red color vibration.

Now pick up the left candle with your left hand and the right candle with your right hand. Say, "I am in perfect psychic balance and I will use this energy only for good."

Replace the candles and focus on the red one for a moment. Take a deep breath and blow out the red candle.

Repeat this procedure with the other six colored candles.

CHAPTER 9

BASIC APPLICATIONS OF YOUR PSYCHIC DEVELOPMENT

THIS CHAPTER COVERS practical applications of your newfound psychic development. Your education and spiritual growth never end. Do not fall into the trap of assuming that you know all you need to and that all you have to do is tune in to yourself if you want some information or experience.

You owe yourself and the universe a karmic responsibility to develop and use your psychic powers for growth. Remember, these are gifts and should never be taken for granted.

PSYCHIC READINGS

As I mentioned before, the most common request for psychic counseling refers to readings. The following information and the following technique will only be beneficial to you when you have mastered the exercises in the previous chapters.

Simply stated, a psychic reading results when you communicate with either your own Higher Self or the Higher Self of another person. You are actually reading the akashic records and this will give you a great deal of information concerning possible future directions, past experiences, and present physical and emotional states.

Present psychically obtained information in a useful, appropriate, and honest fashion. Always remain sensitive to the other person's needs and state of mind so that the other person can integrate and understand this information and use it to enhance self-awareness and self-image. It is inappropriate to place blame or make judgments as a result of the information you receive.

As was noted in Chapter 1, always seek the permission of the person involved before you attempt a reading. Always center yourself and apply protection prior to initiating any procedure. Relax and clear your mind of all thoughts and feelings so that you may function as a clear channel for the information you are about to receive.

There are several ways to receive psychic data. You may sense feelings, hear voices, see images, or visualize symbols. The previous exercises in this book should have helped you determine what your natural psychic mode is.

Do not be concerned about the "right way" to do a psychic reading. There is no one way. The most important thing is your motive and attitude. A true, loving heart, dedication, and discipline are all that is necessary to do a competent psychic reading.

These next three exercises represent different methods of conducting a psychic reading:

1. Sit comfortably, relax, and face the person you will be reading for, who should also be sitting. Surround both of you with protection. Have your subject place his or her hands palms-down directly over your hands, which are palms-up. It is important that you not actually touch your subject's hands. Now ask your Higher Self for assistance. Ask your subject to visualize a relaxing scene, and open yourself up to your subject's vibrations. Let any sensations, feelings, or images flow freely. Share what you receive with your subject. Return to your conscious awareness by taking a deep breath, and then opening your eyes. Instruct your subject to do the same.

To enhance your psychic development it is advisable to switch roles with your subject. Your subject may be a friend or family member.

2. Relax, apply protection, and stand behind your subject, who is sitting comfortably in a chair. Place your palms very close to your subject's head without touching it. Ask your Higher Self for guidance. Open up your third eye by focusing your attention on the space on your forehead between your eyebrows. Note any psychic information or sensations you receive. Share this appropriately with your subject. Return to your conscious awareness in the usual manner.

3. Relax, apply protection, and sit comfortably facing your subject. Have a table with a lit candle on it between you. It can be a colored candle to reflect a special purpose of this reading, if that is appropriate (see Chapter 8). Ask for psychic assistance from your Higher Self, and focus on the flame of the candle. Have your subject ask the following questions several times:

    1. Who was I?

    2. Who am I?

    3. Who will I become?

Meditate on the candle flame and occasionally gaze at your subject's head. Share the information you receive appropriately with your client. End this reading as previously instructed.

◆　◆　◆　◆　◆

PSYCHIC DIAGNOSIS

A psychic diagnosis can be performed on a plant, person, or animal. You do not have to be familiar with the person you are diagnosing. You do not even need to be in the same physical location as the person (or animal or plant) to apply this technique.

In the beginning it is helpful to have another person function as your guide. This person can help you relax and focus your psychic energy before, during, and after the reading. As you become more proficient with your skills, the guide will not be needed. The guide should be sensitive to the psychic, project only positive vibrations, and encourage the psychic to complete the reading accurately. The guide may present the name, address, and age of the person to be read.

Here are some helpful hints to guide you in your initial attempts at psychic diagnosis:

1. Choose a person or object you have some familiarity with. If this person has a disease or an illness you know about, this will allow you to verify your data.

2. Do not select someone who is not living.

3. Refrain from allowing this session to be transformed into a question-and-answer period. The purpose of this exercise is to encourage and sense a steady flow of psychic energy. You can answer the client's questions after the reading.

4. To increase contact with this person, animal, or object simply say, "I'm going to count from one to five. By the time I reach five, I will be in close, comfortable contact with *(name)*" (Count to five.) "My involvement with *(name)* has increased and I am receiving more information."

5. You can reduce contact with this person by saying, "I'm going to count from one to five, and by the time I reach five I will be receiving information at a level that is comfortable for me." (Count to five.) "My involvement has decreased and I am receiving information at a comfortable level."

If you are experiencing difficulty with your reading, the following techniques can help the flow of information:

Visualize your subject in typical daily activities, noting your thoughts, feelings, and actions. These represent your defense mechanisms (ego), which attempt to block psychic growth and development.

Run your hands over your head gently without touching your physical body. Concentrate on the third-eye area.

Imagine that you are your subject, and sense the world from that perspective.

◆　◆　◆　◆　◆

The following exercise will help you sharpen your skills at psychic diagnosis:

Lie down, relax, and apply protection. Ask your Higher Self for guidance in maximizing your ability to tune in to your subject. This helpful data will include knowledge and awareness of your subject's physical, emotional, and spiritual being.

Concentrate on the name, age, and address of your subject. Visualize what your subject looks like and how he or she acts.

Allow your psychic energy to surround this person. Feel the vibrations. Open yourself up to all thoughts, feelings, and impressions.

As you receive information, share it with your subject (if present), your guide (if present), or yourself. Feel free to verbalize what you are learning, even if you are by yourself.

Continue focusing on your subject. Send your psychic energy to this person again. Meditate on your subject for another five minutes. Share the information again, as previously described.

To end this reading, ask your Higher Self to assist you in returning to your conscious awareness. The mental images will now fade. Thank both your Higher Self and your subject for their cooperation.

Let go of any residual thoughts, feelings, and impressions you may have picked up. Breathe deeply and open your eyes, feeling wide awake and filled with positive energy.

◆　◆　◆　◆　◆

HEALING

We all have natural abilities to heal. A psychic cannot cure another person, but can transfer healing energy that can stimulate the receiver's healing centers.

Healing involves the whole person. The principle of balance is used, as healing energy assists in balancing energy centers. A person who becomes imbalanced tends to adapt to this compromised state and begins to accept this as the new mode of living.

When properly applied, healing energy first clears the healer and then the subject. The energy moves directly to the part of the subject's body that shows this imbalance and corrects it. Healing energy energizes and activates the subject's own healing ability.

You can transfer healing energy by touch, words, or sounds. Your subject need not be present. This latter example is called absent healing. Whenever you use your psychic talents, you transfer healing energy, whether you realize it or not.

Healing by touch is very well documented in medical literature. Dolores Krieger, a professor of nursing at New York University, is the pioneer of this method. She was influenced by the work of soul healer Oskar Estebany. Since the 1970s, Krieger has been educating students in this art. More than 50 universities offer courses in therapeutic touch, mostly in their nursing programs.

The ritual of therapeutic touch is reasonably simple. The healer first centers himself or herself, then eases into an altered state of consciousness, concentrating and focusing energies on the healing process. Next, the healer passes his or her hands slowly over the person to be healed, hovering four to six inches (10–15 cm) above the body of the patient, trying to activate the intrinsic energy radiating from the patient's body.

Krieger has utilized therapeutic touch for the treatment of musculoskeletal problems, fevers, inflammation, and many psychosomatic diseases.

Dr. Janet Quinn, of the University of South Carolina, received the first federal grant to study therapeutic touch. In a study she conducted, she had two groups of "healers." One group centered themselves and concentrated on their patients. The control group did not center themselves and simply counted back from 100 as they moved their hands over the patients. These sessions were videotaped. No one watching them could tell the healers from the control group. Patients who received true healing showed a significant drop in anxiety, which was absent from those of the control group.

As already stated, healing doesn't have to involve actually touching the other person. The psychic can work through the aura, as Krieger's work illustrates. You can also physically touch the person to transfer this healing energy.

It is always important to find the cause of the problem or pain, and to work on that cause and permanently remove the symptom. Pain is always the body's way of indicating that something is out of balance. Simply removing the pain alone is not enough. It will return if its cause is not discovered and removed.

A psychic reading can determine why a person does not want to get well. Psychics can assist people to become more positive by using healing energy to remove the fears that may be responsible for their symptoms.

Only someone using psychic abilities will be able to transfer this healing energy. A psychic can do this in a group situation too. And while some people naturally may be able to help a close friend or family member by projecting healing energy, only a trained and competent psychic can assist in healing a stranger.

It's easy to become frustrated when attempting to transfer healing energy. Even the experienced psychic has "dry spells" and finds it impossible to obtain results. Persistence is important, as is maintaining your confidence and not allowing your emotions or ego to block your psychic abilities. Many alternative approaches exist to assist you and expand your choices.

Behavior can very much influence the way your body feels. Here is a list of some examples:

1. Someone dissatisfied on the job and who wants time off may develop a persistent headache or cold.

2. People who find it difficult to communicate with others can develop throat infections.

3. Fear can bring on stomach problems, heart palpitations, and even paralysis.

4. Resentment that builds up can lead to headaches, high blood pressure, and chest pains.

5. Nervous tension can cause painful joints, skin disorders, and speech problems.

6. A loss of hearing has been observed in people who refuse to face the truth.

7. Loneliness can lead to detachment from reality.

8. Depression, irritability, loss of energy, and lethargy can result from an unsympathetic work or home environment.

Psychic diagnosis can quickly pinpoint the cause of these troubles.

Green observed at the top of the head can indicate depression due to lack of creativity. Yellow near the legs may indicate difficulty in walking due to fear. Yellow near the neck area can indicate fear or trouble with communication.

HEALING BY TOUCH

Work on the whole person when transferring healing energy. Your subject may be treated sitting, standing, or lying down.

Have a seated subject lean forward to allow room for your hands between the subject and the back of the chair. Make sure your subject removes glasses and shoes. No other clothing should be removed. Healing energy can go through anything. The only reason for removing shoes is so you can touch your subject's feet.

Have the subject place the palms of the hands face-down on the thighs. Your subject's feet should rest flat on the floor and be slightly apart. Make sure your subject's back is straight. Gently, take the subject's hand. This will give you an initial sense of your subject's energy.

Ask your subject what the problem is, let go of your subject's hand, and stand behind him or her, your hands on the subject's shoulder. Relax, apply protection, and breathe deeply for one minute. Now carry out the following procedures:

Place your index fingers on the bridge of your subject's nose and bring your fingers up the forehead gently, fingers together. Move them over the top of the head, down the back of the head, down the back of their neck, and off at the shoulders. Repeat this three more times, moving more slowly each time.

Place both your thumbs together on the bridge of your subject's nose and repeat the previous procedure.

Put your fingertips on the center of your subject's forehead and stroke outward, stroking the temples and then the ears. Repeat this three times, moving more slowly each time.

Place your fingertips at the top of your subject's nose. Move your stroke upward past the hairline. Repeat this three times.

Now place all your fingers together on your subject's forehead and move your hands downward, not touching your subject's eyes. Gently position your fingers under them and move your fingers off your subject at the ears. Repeat this once.

Stroke your fingers gently down your subject's nose to assist your subject with breathing.

Cup your subject's jaw with one hand on each side of the face to aid in communication.

Place your hands over your subject's ears, move your hands down the back of the ears, down the sides of the neck, and finally off at the shoulder. Repeat this just once.

Place your thumbs at the bottom of your subject's lower jaw. Gently stroke downward to the nape of the subject's neck and flick your thumbs off at the shoulders. Repeat this three times.

Place one hand on either side of your subject's neck vertebrae and gently stroke down and off at the shoulders. This clears negative-energy buildup.

Stand to one side of your subject and place one hand on your subject's breastbone. With the other hand, brush downward from the top of the spine to the bottom, using long, slow movements. Do this three or four times. Brush each side of your subject's spine until the entire back has been brushed, top to bottom. This soothes and calms the nervous system.

Place one hand in front of one of your subject's shoulders and the other hand behind it, so the shoulder is sandwiched between them. Pause a moment, then lift your hands and move them horizontally across your subject. Repeat this until you reach the other shoulder. Move your hands downward and continue to work across your subject's body a hand at a time. Work across the mid-rib region, and move toward the hips. Put one hand on your subject's solar plexus and the other in the small of your sub-ject's back. Pause. This area is a vital energy center that when de-energized can cause backache.

Sit on a low stool in front of your subject. Gently lift one of your subject's hands and place it over the other onto one thigh. Put one of your hands behind your subject's hips and the other on one of your subject's thighs.

Move both hands downward in one long motion and whisk your hands off at the toes. Put your hands on your subject's thigh and move your hands downward to the subject's knee. Pause at the knee joint; then work your way down to the ankles.

Place your subject's foot on your lap and, using both hands, make a counterclockwise motion behind the ankle bone, then around the ankle bone. Stroke your subject's foot from ankle to toes. Gently spread apart the toes and stroke each toe individually, from base to tip. Place your subject's foot between your hands, and pause. Lower the subject's foot to the floor, transfer his or her hands to the finished leg, and repeat the exercise on the other leg. When both legs and feet are completed, put your subject's right hand back on the right leg and the left hand on the left leg.

Stand near your subject's shoulder. Hold the shoulder joint between your hands. Move your hands down your subject's arm and hand, and then, in one motion, move your hands off your subject at the fingertips. Return to your subject's shoulder and work downward from shoulder to elbow. Pause at the elbow, working from the elbow to the wrist. Pause at this joint. Take your subject's hand and spread it out gently. Stroke each finger outward from the base to the fingertip. Put your subject's hand between both of your own, and pause. Put the subject's hand back on his or her leg. Repeat the exercise with the other arm and hand.

Stand behind your subject and place your hands on his or her shoulders. Rest his or her head against yours as you give comfort and compassion.

Stand in front of your subject. Put both your subject's hands together, enclose them in your own, and hold them for a few seconds. You are encircling them with energy by this action and making sure they retain the energy you have transferred to them. Thank your subject for coming. Place your subject's right hand back on the right leg and left hand on the left leg. Move away. Do not hover over your subject at this time. The subject needs to adjust and to clear the space. The energy you gave becomes your subject's. Tell your subject to stand and stretch into the space when the time to do so feels right.

Your final action, when your subject has left and before you touch another person, is to brush your hands together to signify the finish. This ensures that you do not transfer your subject's energy to yourself or your next subject. Finally, wash your hands.

◆　◆　◆　◆　◆

When healing, always work downward. By moving your hands in this direction, you will be able to sense vibrations and temperature changes. Your hands may actually quiver when your healing energy is transferred to your subject. Remember, whatever you do with your subject cannot worsen your subject's condition. The worst that can happen is nothing.

Do not walk in front of a client during a healing session. Your own energy will not be drained as a result of this session if you are properly grounded and protected (see Chapter 4).

LASER HEALING

When a psychic concentrates energy into an intense beam of light, this is called laser healing. This should be used for short periods only, as it is very intense.

The procedure is as follows:

Your subject sits opposite you. Take your subject's hand for a minute or two to tune in to his or her energy.

Begin transmitting a fine blue light and a green light of energy from your third-eye area to your subject's crown chakra, on top of the head. Hold the two beams of light until you feel a tingling, cold, or warm sensation on your forehead.

When your feel this, add to these beams the proper color to reflect the problem. Mauve is added to aid communication, yellow to lessen fear, green for creativity, and blue to combat depression.

Now move these three beams of light down from the forehead to the affected area. Hold them in one position for 10 seconds and then fan them out over the area.

Move these three beams about 12 inches over your subject's head and combine them with your subject's aura (see Chapter 3). Fan these light beams downward to your subject's feet.

Meditate for three minutes without touching your subject. Place your subject's hands together, move away, and then brush your hands against your thighs.

◆　◆　◆　◆　◆

This technique activates healing energy while revitalizing both the sender and receiver.

ABSENT HEALING

This form of healing is done without your subject present. You must always have your subject's permission to initiate healing. Try to let your subject know the exact time you will be conducting this healing exercise.

Absent healing can be successfully carried out in any part of the world. This energy travels at the speed of light, so results can occur immediately. It is ideal to use a photograph of your subject as a reference point. The name and address on a piece of paper will also work.

The following exercise is an example of absent healing:

Sit quietly, relax, and apply protection. Breathe deeply and look at the photograph or name for one minute. Now stare out in front of you and create an image of your subject.

Now begin to send color energy. To determine which color to send, simply ask your Higher Self to assist you. Pink can be transmitted to minimize emotional difficulties, green for creativity, yellow for courage, and so on. If you do not know what color to send, transmit green first, then blue, and finally a combination of the remaining colors (see Chapter 8).

If you have photographs of several different people, do this process with each picture. Do the same with names on paper, if that is all you have to work from.

◆　◆　◆　◆　◆

As with all other forms of psychic healing, absent healing is perfectly safe. You cannot heal a person who doesn't want to be well. Your efforts will usually help your subject become positive and strong.

GROUP ABSENT HEALING

The following exercise is very successful with a group of several healers:

Sit in a healing circle, one member functioning as the group leader.

The leader asks each member to meditate and bring up his or her psychic healing energy. The leader then connects this energy to his or her own.

The leader repeats the name and location of all persons to be healed, passing around any photographs to each group member.

The group healing energy is now directed clockwise around the group and projected out to the recipient.

◆　◆　◆　◆　◆

Each future meeting of this group adds to the healing energy previously transmitted. Anyone in the group can access this group-healing energy for personal use without causing disruption to the others.

BALANCING ENERGY CENTERS

Each energy center has its own color and moves in a clockwise direction. These are labeled as follows:

1. The inspiration center is located in the upper part of the head, and is blue.

2. The communication center is located in the lower head and neck, and is mauve.

3. The emotional center is located in the heart area, and is pink laced with red.

4. The courage center is located in the solar plexus region, and is yellow.

5. The creativity center is located in the tailbone, and is green. This center includes the feet and legs.

The following exercise will help you see whether these centers are in balance:

Relax, apply protection, and ask your Higher Self to tune in to the blue of inspiration. Check the blue in its own center and follow the blue line moving down into the communication center. Check the blue energy moving through the mauve and down to the emotional center. Check the blue as it spirals around the emotional center and then moves down to the courage center. Check as it spirals around the courage center and moves down to the creativity center, including the legs and feet.

If you sense any imbalance in blue energy, focus on the blue energy from your third-eye area and keep this focus until you sense that your subject's blue energy is back in balance.

Repeat this procedure with mauve, beginning in the communication center. Check the mauve in its own center first, then travel upward to check inspiration, downward to communication, down and around emotion, down and around courage, down and around creativity, including the legs and feet, and back to the communication center.

If you sense an imbalance, pause, then send mauve from your mid-forehead center to the point affected until the imbalance is corrected.

The next center is emotions (pink/red). Do the same procedure. Repeat the procedure for courage (yellow), then creativity (green).

Next, from your mid-forehead to 12 inches (30 cm) above your subject's head, send a beam of all colors. Sweep down past all centers to below your subject's feet and back up to above your subject's head. Switch off the contact by sensing the colors fading. Ask the colors to stand and shake and stretch in their own space. Move away from your subject and brush your hands together to disconnect.

◆ ◆ ◆ ◆ ◆

SELF-HEALING

The following exercise will balance and energize your psychic healing centers:

Meditate upon arising, apply protection, and check each center, as in the previous exercise.

Progressively relax your body. Transmit your natural healing energy from your toes to the top of your head. Gently flex the muscles in your body as this healing energy and feeling of relaxation spreads.

Be alert to any sounds or communication from your Higher Self.

Concentrate on a spot just above the top of your head—you may sense a color, or visualize a relaxing place. As you watch the image, one color will stand out from the rest. This is the color you need for the day. Your aura needs this color. Put your hands on the areas that feel imbalanced. Sense the color pulsating through your hands into the area. While transferring the color, try to sense why the imbalance has occurred.

Should the discomfort return during the day, use your hands to put the same color in the area and it will be relieved. Use this information in choosing your wardrobe for the day.

◆　◆　◆　◆　◆

BALANCING YOUR FLOW OF ENERGY

The following exercise will adjust the energy flow in and around your body:

Stand up straight, feet apart. Stretch your hands above your head.

Hold this position and count to 15.

Relax and take a few deep breaths. Your energy is now balanced.

◆　◆　◆　◆　◆

Always remember the advantage of color healing. Use blue for harmony and relief from physical discomforts. Green is used for inner peace and harmony. Just by using these two colors, beginners will greatly reduce physical and emotional distress.

CHAPTER 10

OTHER APPLICATIONS OF YOUR PSYCHIC DEVELOPMENT

ONE OF THE many advantages of developing your psychic awareness is the effect your growth will have on others as well as yourself. The more you tap into the "psychic awareness superhighway," the greater your sense of inner peace and harmony. You will experience a oneness that only those undergoing this type of growth can understand.

As your psychic gifts expand, you will find yourself able to tune in to other people's energy to assist them in their growth. This form of absent psychic development will not require the physical presence of the other person.

IMPROVING RELATIONSHIPS

The ability to improve your relationships in a "win-win" way is one of the greatest advantages of your psychic development. Without trying to manipulate others, you can foster an increase in the quality of any type of relationship. By turning to your newly developed intuition, you will be able to diagnose the real problem quickly and have your Higher Self assist you in finding a solution. Love is always the most important factor in your personal relationships. Your Higher Self will aid you in fostering both love of self and love of others.

Here are some simple examples of how you can improve your relationships by using your newly developed psychic abilities:

1. Use your intuition to help you develop positive relationships. Your Higher Self will aid you in removing guilt and other "self-defeating patterns" that have placed unwanted blocks in your path. Your intuition will also help you focus your psychic energy on establishing fulfilling relationships with others.

2. Keep your energy balanced at all times. The exercises in this book will help you achieve this goal. If your own psychic energy is compromised, you won't be able to get through to your Higher Self or others. Even when you do balance your energy, you must recognize that others may not be in a position to receive your signals. Be patient.

3. Make relationship goals a top priority. Concentrate all your psychic energy on one issue at a time. Do this nonjudgmentally. It is important that your motives be pure and that you really want the relationship to improve. Do not use these techniques to patronize or control others.

4. Refrain from using relationship difficulties as an excuse to avoid other issues. Nothing is more destructive to the development of psychic abilities than *excusitis*. Empowerment is a prerequisite to psychic growth. Making excuses, procrastination, and displacement of anger or responsibilities have no place in psychic development.

5. Practice loving others and letting go of all negativity in your environment. You'd be surprised what effect love has. Sending out positive energy to "negative" people can have a calming effect, if done with your psychic energy. I do not mean to imply you may allow yourself to be victimized by others. You must also be able to release the negativity projected on you by others or even yourself. The balancing, centering, and protection techniques described in this book will assist you with this goal.

6. End relationships that simply are not working. This is a very important principle of empowerment. No matter how hard you may try, some people just project negative energy and will only bring you

down in the long run. It is quite common to stay in dysfunctional relationships too long, due to insecurity. Be it a relationship with a spouse, child, parent, or "best friend," if your experience and Higher Self inform you that there is simply no hope, end the relationship.

The following exercise will clear the energy paths between you and others:

Relax, apply protection, and breathe deeply for one minute.

Visualize meeting another person in a relaxing environment. Take a few minutes to visualize the details of the room or place of this get-together.

Invite the person to enter and sit down next to you. Offer refreshments and anything you think will help the other person feel comfortable.

Now imagine your end of the conversation. Imagine that you are expressing yourself freely. Perceive the other person replying to you. Do this for five minutes.

If you have difficulty with Step 4, repeat it later in the day or the following day when the signal is clearer. End your visualization in the standard manner.

◆ ◆ ◆ ◆ ◆

This exercise will establish a better connection with that person. It is a type of "thought forming" (see Chapter 7) and will lead to more "accidental" meetings with this soul.

Your intuition will improve and you will "know" what is on this person's mind. Interestingly, the person will also improve the psychic connection with you. Remember that these approaches are not meant to be used as a quick fix for problems. They are designed to develop relationships over a long period of time for mutual spiritual growth.

Other suggestions for improving your relationships by using your psychic abilities are:

1. Realize that all relationships exist to teach you some lesson in life. There is a karmic purpose to both good and bad relationships. Nothing happens by accident. When you learn to make lemonade from life's lemons, you are growing spiritually. When faced with a difficult relationship, ask your Higher Self what the lesson is.

2. All relationships are psychically created. The new physics teaches that you create your reality. As long as you continue to ignore a universal law of karma, it will repeat itself until you adequately deal with it. The faster you learn this and the more you grow spiritually, the sooner your relationships will improve. You may not be able to change another person, but you can alter your thoughts, feelings, and psychic projections about that person. That is all you need to do to meet your karmic responsibilities.

3. Write about your relationship exercises and their outcome in your psychic journal. This will help you keep track of your progress. Every time you write about someone in your journal, you are sending psychic energy to that person. Healing a relationship's wounds can occur by just this simple technique alone. This works better when you meditate on your journal entry.

4. Believe in yourself and always project confidence and optimism. Positive projection techniques work. Use self-hypnosis or meditation to work on yourself. The energy you send out will be returned to you. You will attract into your life souls that reflect your own spiritual development. You have done this already throughout your life.

5. Trust in your psychic powers. You will always add to the strength of your psychic energy projections if you believe in your abilities. Your Higher Self will always relate the truth to you. It is your responsibility to learn to trust it.

6. Practice visualization techniques. These exercises are the most efficient way I know to foster the development of positive relationships. Visualization allows you a wide range of ways to create any kind of environment and response you like in order to facilitate healthy relationships. Have fun with these approaches and be prepared to reap the rewards.

ATTRACTING PARTNERS INTO YOUR LIFE

The following visualization exercise will assist you in attracting a quality partner:

Relax, apply protection, and breathe deeply for one minute. Create an accurate portrait of yourself, one honestly representing who you are today. Visualize your aura and psychic energy and imagine this energy pulsating around your physical body.

Now imagine a portrait of a person you want to attract. It should be someone you do not know and have never seen. Take your time and make the picture as accurate as you can. Include hair color, physique, eye color, height, and weight. Also include interests, education, family background, and occupation. Now perceive the aura and psychic energy pulsating around the person's body.

Imagine your aura and psychic energy being sent out and meeting this person's energy. Meditate on this interaction for five minutes. This works better with New Age music playing in the background.

Ask your Higher Self to help you. What can you do to facilitate this meeting? How can you make it happen sooner? Ask your Higher Self these and other questions to speed up this process.

◆　◆　◆　◆　◆

One of the goals of this exercise is to train you to look at yourself realistically. Another is to determine realistically the type of person you want to meet. The more realistic your goals and the higher the quality of your own energy and psychic development, the more satisfied you will be with the results.

This exercise will help you to foster a relationship with the person you attract into your life as a result of the previous exercise:

Relax, apply protection, and breathe deeply. Visualize a symbol you associate with love. It can be anything, but should not be a sexual image. Some people imagine a cup overflowing, symbolizing love. Whatever you find comfortable and meaningful will work.

Now imagine a beam of pure love energy emanating from your heart. Direct this beam of love toward your partner, a person you already have a loving relationship with. Ask your Higher Self to assist you.

Imagine the love symbol you visualized earlier responding to this projection of energy. For example, the liquid in the overflowing cup might vibrate with energy and move rapidly as it pours from the cup, resulting in a feeling of pure love between yourself and your partner.

Now imagine a golden cord linking your heart to your partner's. See this golden cord pulsate and glow. Visualize holding out your arms. See your partner running toward you and hugging you. Do not create a sexual scene, just a loving scene.

Stay with this scene for at least five minutes. End this exercise when your Higher Self directs you to do so.

◆　◆　◆　◆　◆

CREATING ABUNDANCE

The next application of your psychic development deals with the creation of abundance in the material world. You might think that this is some violation of a universal or karmic law. It is not.

There is nothing wrong with your materially benefiting from your psychic development, as long as it is not at the expense of someone else. I refer to this as "karmic capitalism." If it were not for this principle, few would dedicate themselves professionally to this field. They would simply treat psychic development as a hobby, and the universe would be denied the very services and energy projection it needs to evolve positively.

My own case is a perfect example. I spent a lot of time, money, and effort in being trained as a dentist. After two years of full-time dental practice, with a part-time past-life-regression hypnotherapy pursuit, I reversed the two. During the next 11 years I practiced dentistry only 10 hours a week, while devoting 40–60 hours to my hypnotherapy practice.

If it were not for the material success of my hypnotherapy practice, I could not possibly have made this transition. You do not need to make the radical change I did, but you most certainly are entitled to earn a good living as a psychic, if that is your career path, and to attract material benefits into your life.

When you alter how you think, feel, and react to the material world, you change the quality of the energy you send and receive. By eliminating fears of financial inadequacy, for example, you will attract better financial opportunities into your life. This can help a salesperson increase weekly or monthly sales. Another possibility is to generate better offers on a car or home that you might be trying to sell.

The following recommendations will help you to create abundance in the material world:

1. Accept the concept that you have the psychic ability to create abundance. This relates to the self-image issue mentioned several times before. You must believe in yourself and that what you are doing is right. It is important to eliminate the "out there" form of thinking of abundance and bring it "in here."

By asking your Higher Self for assistance, you can rely on the fact that your abundance will only improve if it is meant to do so. Prosperity is produced by your Higher Self. It is not an isolated event.

2. Select a higher value over a lower one. This does not mean you should become obsessed with money or prices. It is a principle I call "realistic idealism." You pick and choose your goals. Sometimes an endeavor will be associated with no material gain. By eliminating clutter and petty materialistic concerns, you can free your Higher Self to help you with the big picture.

A good example is a patient of mine who had a natural interest in floral arrangement. She wanted to develop this talent into a hobby. She accessed her Higher Self and used her natural creativity and psychic powers to become very adept at this art. Shortly afterwards, friends of hers began to hire her to design arrangements for family and professional gatherings. During the next 18 months, she established a lucrative full-time business as a floral designer, making more money than her CPA husband. She has never been happier professionally. Equally important, the universe and her clients benefited greatly from her talents.

3. Accept the fact that your mind has all the information and techniques available to create abundance for you. When you use self-hypnosis or meditation daily, you are tapping into your Higher Self. This perfect, all-knowing aspect of yourself will patiently teach you how to attain your materialistic goals ethically.

You must trust your intuitive powers and Higher Self, and you must also be open to receiving those rewards in whatever form they arrive.

Your "gut feelings," "hunches," and insights will now work overtime to help you.

One procedure you must master is concentration. Without focused concentration, you will be spinning your psychic wheels needlessly and inefficiently. Prosperity is first created in the mind. Your subconscious will then execute a plan to make this idea reality.

4. Accept the unusual and expect the unexpected. There are no boundaries or limitations on what your mind can create and accomplish. Prosperity has a way of arriving when you least expect it. It will require hard work and dedication, but the quantum leaps you will experience in your net worth will appear to be unexpected and most unusual. This is part of the fun of karmic capitalism.

5. Imagination creates an abundance mentality. Imagination implies more than just the usual imagery. By developing your psychic awareness, you will create your abundance with the help of your Higher Self. You are your only limitation.

Your defense mechanisms (ego) may have always said, "I don't have the right talents to make more money." They may also say, "I guess I'll just never have enough money." This is all going to change as you raise your psychic awareness and self-image. Your Higher Self will assist you in the necessary reprogramming to accomplish these goals.

You will develop optimism and a positive sense about yourself based on new experience. Positive attitudes breed prosperity. People always gather around others who project confidence. You can see this in your work environment, at a lecture, or in any public meeting place. Your new confidence will make it easier for you to create abundance. You will keep this prosperity and will foster it because your self-image is higher and you know you deserve this success. All this will begin once you develop your psychic awareness.

AN EXERCISE TO ATTRACT MONEY INTO YOUR LIFE

Relax, apply protection, and breathe deeply. Create an image in your mind of a specific material goal. This may be a certain amount of money.

Meditate on this goal and write it in your psychic journal with today's date. Visualize a check for this exact amount of money being written to you for goods or services you sold.

Mentally receive it with confidence and see yourself depositing these funds in your bank. Next, focus on opening your bank statement a few weeks later with this deposit reflected. Meditate on this image for several minutes. End this exercise in the usual manner.

◆ ◆ ◆ ◆ ◆

YOUR ATTITUDE TOWARD MONEY

If you think money is evil or that only bad or unethical people become wealthy, you are defeating your abundance goals before you get started. It is always your responsibility to grow spiritually, to expect the best, and to feel you deserve prosperity in every form.

Developing your psychic abilities allows you to coordinate the priceless reserves of your Higher Self. Affirmations or desires alone will not work. You must believe in your "heart of hearts" that you deserve this positive bounty, and you must send out the appropriate energy to make this a reality.

Learn about yourself. Find out what your beliefs and expectations are. Note these in your psychic journal. Change them if necessary. This isn't as hard as it sounds. Eliminate any blocks that held you back in the past by choosing on a subconscious level images and goals that will benefit you.

Here are some suggestions to assist you in changing your attitudes toward money:

1. Focus on what you have, while eliminating any tendency to complain about what you don't have. Use the monitoring exercise in Chapter 5 to assist you in this goal. Every time you catch yourself falling into familiar, dysfunctional thought processes, meditate on the correct viewpoint. Focus on such statements as "I deserve abundance" or "My desires for prosperity are well within my karmic rights."

2. Meditate or use self-hypnosis to ask your Higher Self for specific suggestions about how to improve your attitude toward money.

Visualize yourself writing down any counterproductive tendencies and erasing them. Another technique is to visualize index cards with these counterproductive tendencies written out on them. Visualize them attached to helium-filled balloons that are lifting up into the air and floating permanently away.

3. Visualize your subconscious projecting your abundance goals into positive psychic energy. See this energy connecting with mechanisms that will transform these goals into a reality.

4. You must first have a money goal. Write it down. Keep it in mind. Remember, everything in the material world begins on another plane. Use the mental plane to assist your subconscious in formulating the necessary psychic energy and projecting it correctly to create this reality.

5. Always thank your Higher Self for its efforts and assistance. Be thankful and not demanding or condescending when dealing with your Higher Self.

These recommendations and techniques are not merely wishful thinking. Money and other material rewards are not created from thin air. Your intuition can help you, but you are solely responsible for accessing your psychic gifts to attain these goals.

Do not attempt frivolous goals with these methods. You will fail repeatedly if you do. If you need a job, visualizing one is not enough. You must still go out and look for one and possibly face several rejections before you land the job you desire.

Always request assistance from your Higher Self. I have already presented several exercises on how to impress a job interviewer. Use these visual-imagery techniques daily. Do not forget to document these attempts in your psychic journal. Meditate on this journal and you will find these positive results happening sooner.

You can meditate on a specific job, career change, or anything else that will facilitate your abundance goals. Always keep your motives pure. It is not selfish to seek money and possessions, but it is selfish to do so at someone else's expense or to get back at another person. You may succeed in the short run, but you will hurt yourself in the long run.

Here is a simple exercise you can practice to help you discover your life's work:

Relax, apply protection, and breathe deeply for one minute. Mentally stand in front of a blackboard and gently request your Higher Self to list your current talents and abilities.

Now list the types of jobs you have held in the past. Finally, list the job or profession you would like to have now.

Meditate on these lists for five minutes. Now turn the blackboard over. The answer to your question of a career choice will appear.

◆   ◆   ◆   ◆   ◆

Practice this exercise several times if you do not receive an answer. Note all results in your psychic journal. Other techniques that work are the precognition and forecasting exercises from Chapter 7.

PERSONAL GROWTH

By far the most important application of your psychic development is toward your own personal growth. As you grow spiritually your psychic abilities will be enhanced accordingly. Other areas where you can expect an increase are your self-image, creativity, resistance to stress, performance in any task, and ability to learn.

This creates a chain reaction. By improving the mind-body-spirit connection, you create a boundless, unstoppable momentum. Your results will have practical applications. This won't mean much if you aren't happy.

In my Los Angeles office I see many wealthy, famous, and powerful people. They have everything they want, except for one thing: They are miserable. It may be difficult to comprehend how people with so many advantages could be so unhappy.

These celebrity patients do not request my hypnotherapy services to brag about how great their life is. Who hasn't heard about the dysfunctional, self-defeating behavior of the rich and famous?

Apply this to your own life. Motivation and psychic awareness are the most important qualities you can have. The rest is simply a matter of time and application. Solving personal problems is not merely a nice thing to do. It is your duty to yourself and the universe to grow continually.

Psychic development is not a magic pill. It is a marvelous tool you have at your disposal (if you choose to learn to use it) and a powerful way to nurture your subconscious to grow into that unlimited soul you were meant to be.

Here are some hints that will assist you in improving your self-confidence:

1. *Use your creative abilities.* Your talent for visual imagery combined with your psychic awareness will unlock an energy flow that will result in goals accomplished. As you achieve more, you feel even better about yourself, which leads to more confidence as you begin work on additional goals. In this way, you can create your reality. The world you live in begins in your mind.

2. *Practice discipline.* It is impossible to attain a desirable goal without sticking to a plan. This conscientiousness is another name for discipline. Only self-confident people can live consistently disciplined lives. Discipline will seem tedious at first, but will become ingrained as your self-confidence increases.

Many of my patients complain about procrastination. Almost without exception, it is not the task at hand that is the problem. The difficulty lies in beginning the task. This same principle applies to discipline. Eventually you will look forward to tasks with tedious details because you know you can do them and you have too much self-confidence to invite the repercussions of not doing them.

3. *Create optimism in every situation.* Most people go through life feeling the cup is half empty. I work with many patients who, at first, don't feel they have a drop of water in the cup. They rationalize their attitude as a result of past frustrations and failures.

What they fail to realize is that they created this failure reality, and that whatever the mind creates it can uncreate. By consistently thinking optimistically and by projecting that energy, you increase the efficiency of your psychic abilities and your chance to help make your desires come true. You have absolutely nothing to lose and everything to gain from this approach.

4. *Replace overly rational thought processes with an open, intuitive attitude.*

When you suspend rational thoughts (the defense mechanisms or ego), you are enhancing your creative and psychic talents. The last thing you want to encourage is left-brain (rational) activity, because this will push away any attempt at psychic development and any improvement to your self-image.

The rational mind likes "business as usual," and this is counterproductive to spiritual growth and change of any kind. Your Higher Self will assist you, but in the beginning you will need to monitor your thoughts and catch yourself every time you find yourself giving in to rational thoughts at inopportune moments.

5. *Assess the words you use in your everyday conversations.* This also applies to conversations with yourself. Catch yourself when you say, "I am getting fat," or "I just can't seem to get anywhere." These words program your subconscious and lower your self-confidence.

Practice the monitoring exercises in Chapter 7 to end this tendency. You can say to yourself, "I am not lazy, weak, stupid, or afraid." Reaffirm your strengths and recognize that these undercutting remarks originate from the ego, whose purpose is to prevent your self-image from growing.

You can easily reverse negative programming by telling yourself, "I am intelligent." You can say, "I look great in this outfit." Positive statements like these will become second nature as you raise your self-confidence level.

Admit to making mistakes, instead of degrading yourself over them. To err is human, but not necessarily a sign of stupidity. This shift in the way you speak will actually exert an effect on your life.

6. *Curb your natural tendency to doubt yourself.* Doubts prevent growth. You cannot function as a self-confident soul by constantly doubting everything you do or say, or every decision you make. Eliminate the words and expressions "perhaps," "maybe," "I'll take that under advisement," and "I can't make a decision." There are times when you will need more information to make a choice, but these will be the minority of situations you will face in your daily life.

AN EXERCISE TO INCREASE YOUR SELF-CONFIDENCE

Before beginning this exercise I suggest you take a mental inventory of who you are. Practice the earlier exercises in this chapter on improving relationships and creating abundance and review the results before you begin this one. You may also want to review your psychic journal to get an overall inventory of what you think and how you feel about yourself. When you have done this, try the following exercise:

Sit comfortably, relax, apply protection, and breathe deeply. Visualize yourself in your favorite serene environment. It may be the beach, a park, or a cabin in the woods. Add to this the sounds of nature and the time of year you enjoy most.

Imagine walking along in your favorite surroundings while looking up at the sky. Notice that a rainbow has appeared and focus your attention on the colors. You see red, yellow, blue, green, orange, purple, and violet.

As you stare at this rainbow, realize that you can accomplish anything you want to as long as you can see the rainbow. The rainbow doesn't need to be present for you to accomplish your goal, but if it is there, it assures a successful outcome to any quest.

Sit down now and think of the kind of person you would like to become. Review personality traits, health issues, finances, and relationships. Focus on specific goals and aspects of your personality. Look up again and see the rainbow. You are now able to accomplish the goal of becoming who you want to be.

Imagine a large television screen in front of you. Project the ideal you on the right side of this large TV.

This is called a split-screen effect, because you will now project an image of how you are on the left side. Imagine yourself adjusting the fine-tuning knobs.

As you adjust the TV, the ideal image of you becomes crystal clear, while the current image of you goes out of focus and then disappears completely.

Look up one more time and note the presence of the rainbow. The ideal image of you is now your new reality.

Meditate on this image for at least five minutes with soothing New Age music playing in the background.

Finally, breathe deeply, open up your eyes, and say, "I am confident. I am in charge of my life and I now claim my power to improve my confidence level every day." End your trance as usual.

◆　◆　◆　◆　◆

USING PSYCHIC DEVELOPMENT TO FORMULATE LEARNING

Another application of your psychic development will be to speed up the learning process. We learn better when we study in meditative or hypnotic levels. The right brain is far more efficient than the left brain. Your psychic development is a right-brain function.

The following suggestions will help you to improve your learning ability through the application of your psychic development:

1. Tell yourself positive things about your intelligence and ability to learn.

2. Always use meditation or self-hypnosis exercises before doing any reading or other activity requiring concentration.

3. Visualize yourself successfully attaining a goal. This might be an "A" on an exam, or some other desirable goal.

4. Ask your Higher Self for assistance in facilitating your learning.

5. Program yourself with the following statements when you are in a relaxed state:

A. "I am a good student and enjoy studying."

B. "I remember what I learned."

C. "My mind will give me any information I desire."

D. "Learning is fun and easy."

E. "My intuition allows me to learn faster."

F. "My mind will always present information to me when I need it."

You can add to this list. I highly recommend making a tape and playing it prior to any study periods.

SOLVING PERSONAL PROBLEMS WITH YOUR INTUITION

I like to look at problems as growth opportunities. You karmically choose every problem in your life, and you do this to learn from each situation so you may grow spiritually. You can handle these learning opportunities better when you ask your Higher Self for guidance.

In attempting to solve personal problems, you are going to have to obtain knowledge in some form. Sources of knowledge are everywhere. One is telepathic contact with the minds of others. Another is the accumulated experience, knowledge, and documents recorded by society. The third is the Higher Self, which is perfect and all-knowing.

I prefer the last source for the simple reason that it is perfect and a part of your psychic energy. It is empowering to solve your own problems with your own psychic energy. It is mere co-dependence to use the other sources of knowledge.

The following are some simple rules to assist you in solving your personal problems:

1. Always ask your Higher Self for guidance.

2. Do not be in a rush for an answer. Be patient and wait as long as necessary for the solution.

3. Always present a problem to your intuitive mind as specifically as possible.

4. Do your homework. Research the situation as thoroughly as you can.

5. After you have reviewed your research data, meditate on the problem.

6. Put the issue out of your mind, unless it is an emergency, and go back to it the next day.

7. When in doubt about any of these rules, ask your Higher Self for guidance.

These rules are designed to sidestep your conscious (rational) mind and go right to your subconscious. Your subconscious can access your Higher Self and give you a fast and desirable solution to your problem.

Waiting the 24 hours is not a form of procrastination. This allows the Higher Self to assess the problem globally and communicate the solution to the subconscious mind. You will often experience the answer in the form of an insight. This insight may occur the following day.

CHAPTER 11

OVERCOMING OBSTACLES TO YOUR PSYCHIC DEVELOPMENT

EVERYTHING IS RELATIVE. What is East to one person may be West to someone else. The only obstacles in the world are the ones we create. Developing your psychic abilities can facilitate your spiritual growth by leaps and bounds. If you allow potential obstacles to interfere with your spiritual growth, you will miss these opportunities. This chapter will assist you in overcoming these obstacles.

You have free will. Free will allows you to grow spiritually, stay the same, or regress negatively and dysfunctionally. You can adapt any way you choose to the continual flow of information you are exposed to daily.

You can choose to remember what you learn and observe, or you can discard any data you receive. Your subconscious permanently stores everything your five senses and your psychic abilities teach you.

All people, events, and actions leave an energy trail that is detectable psychically. A properly trained subconscious mind can tap into this energy. Using the exercises and techniques in this book with discipline, proper motivation, and confidence can give you such a properly trained mind.

Knowledge is actually part of you and it never disappears. It is a component of the aura, the subconscious mind (soul), and the Higher Self. Knowledge is more than mere information.

Your intelligence, ethics, and level of spiritual growth determine what you do with knowledge. Your defense mechanisms, on the other hand, try constantly to prevent you from assimilating any knowledge that will result in change.

THE EGO

The universe is filled with obstacles. The strongest is your own ego. The reason for this is simple. Your ego is a part of you. It lives with you and contributes to your thoughts. It censors what you do and say.

Your ego has only been with you in this lifetime. It will die when your physical body crosses into spirit. Your soul or subconscious is eternal. As pure energy it cannot be destroyed—not even when you die.

THE SUBCONSCIOUS

Since your subconscious has been with you throughout all your past lives, it knows you well. This knowledge and experience are no match for the defense mechanisms. The subconscious is a computer that is programmed daily. The world we live in has more negativity than positive energy.

You must control this programming or you will lose your greatest asset in overcoming these obstacles. Without the proper use of your subconscious you cannot access your Higher Self. This book trains you to program your subconscious positively and to establish a regular communication with your Higher Self.

As a young child you had no difficulty making contact with your Higher Self. You also didn't have many obstacles to that contact, because your mind and body were growing fast and you exhibited a natural thirst for knowledge and change.

At around the age of six or so you began to get from society negativity in the form of guilt, shame, and "you-can't-do-that." When you give in to this brainwashing, you lose the natural connection with your Higher Self.

This results in the creation of the greatest obstacle to your psychic development and, unless you undergo specific spiritual-growth training, your ego will control your thoughts, feelings, and behavior.

By using this book, you are reversing this trend. You can understand your karmic purpose and recognize the connection you have with other souls. This will allow you to rise above these self-made obstacles.

REPRESSED KNOWLEDGE

The universe has plenty of knowledge to share. In order for you to acquire it, you must be open to receiving it. Society does not promote this openness. Most Americans, for example, do not believe in reincarnation and American society looks askance at this truth.

As a soul you desire spiritual growth. Part of that growth requires a certain knowledge. Much of what you were taught as truth is incorrect. You cannot grow unless you obtain this knowledge. One of your obstacles is society.

Many people have been persecuted and killed for beliefs that were in opposition to society's "norms." It is your right and your duty as a psychically developed soul to access your Higher Self and seek the truth. Do not be concerned about the opinion of others. This is part of your empowerment.

Without a personal belief system, you are nothing but an animal. Your beliefs are formed from many sources. The best source is your Higher Self. Universal truths do not change.

You are only limited by your beliefs. This obstacle can easily be removed by psychic development. Society cannot prevent you from communicating with your Higher Self. Only you can do that. Even if you were put to death for your beliefs, you would reincarnate and continue your quest for knowledge and truth in a future life.

Opening up your mind to all possibilities expands your levels of consciousness. Using meditation and self-hypnosis facilitates this openness and establishes the all-important connection with your Higher Self.

Many spiritual-growth opportunities are available to the psychically developed soul, but you must look for them. When you accept the concept of a soul and a Higher Self, you enter a different universe, where anything is possible and spiritual growth is the norm.

PSYCHIC FOUNDATIONS

In order to perfect your psychic skills you need to focus your concentration. If you scatter your interests, you will fail at these exercises. I realize that I have presented dozens of techniques and exercises. My purpose has been to give you a broad spectrum to choose from in order to find your niche. You will not be as successful with some techniques as with others. Find your own style, then concentrate on procedures that appeal to you.

Scattered energy is another obstacle to your psychic foundation. By applying yourself diligently to certain techniques and growing psychically, you will begin to appreciate how these principles relate to psychic development. If you try a wide spectrum, you will find the ones that work for you. You must have knowledge and experience to make these choices, so that they become part of your spiritual growth and not another obstacle.

You need a solid foundation if you are to succeed at building something lasting. This is why I include self-healing and balancing exercises in this book, and why I repeatedly emphasize the importance of establishing and maintaining contact with your Higher Self. This is your best foundation and the solution to any obstacle the universe might place in your path.

For the most part, you need to do these exercises alone. It is important that you allot quiet time for meditation or self-hypnosis. Your emotions take away from your psychic foundation. Thoughts are even worse.

Reflection on who you are and on your present path will greatly aid you in your quest for a solid foundation. This is one purpose of your psychic journal. It details your progress. Meditate with it as I have suggested throughout this book.

KARMIC OBSTACLES

These detours to your spiritual path are rarely seen. They may be felt as a sense of urgency, depression, or desperation. Your psychic foundation will assist you in dealing with these challenges.

You may very well be involved with someone you knew in a previous life in an unpleasant way. This karmic debt does not have to result in your being victimized. By accessing your Higher Self you can cleanse this negativity away.

A little-known aspect of karma exists that I call the principle of forgiveness. It states that by changing your motives, thoughts, and actions you can erase a lot of accumulated negative karma at one time. In other words, you do not have to correct every single flaw or error in each of your past lives. If that were required, nobody would complete the karmic cycle.

Nothing but yourself stands in the way of overcoming karmic obstacles. Making excuses will not rectify the situation. It only makes it worse. The karmic "buck" stops here.

A certain amount of self-control is necessary for you to achieve spiritual growth. This is part of your discipline. Most people show good self-control in their professional lives, but fail to apply this principle to personal relationships.

To grow spiritually and maximize the development of your psychic abilities, you must exhibit this self-control in all aspects of your life. Lack of self-control is an obstacle to psychic development. This is a karmic choice, so it becomes a karmic obstacle as well.

The exercise I am about to present deals with overcoming obstacles by taking personal control over your life. Consider these questions and refer to your psychic journal as you answer them.

Relax, apply protection, and breathe deeply. Meditate on each of the following questions and allow your Higher Self to assist you in finding the answers:

What circumstances exert the major influences on your life at this time?

Are any of these situations self-imposed? If they are self-imposed, how can you eliminate the obstacles they present?

Categorize these obstacles into personal and professional areas. Which would you like to improve? Design a plan to do so.

What kind of balance is needed to deal constructively with each of these obstacles?

How can you achieve this balance?

What unnecessary obligations do you have in your life at this time?

How are you going to correct these?

When will you start this?

How will you begin?

What new goals can you work on once these obstacles are removed?

Where will your life be in six months? In one year? In five years?

◆   ◆   ◆   ◆   ◆

Log these questions and your responses in your psychic journal. Re-evaluate these questions and answers every two months and modify your goals accordingly.

CONCLUSION

Psychic development leads to spiritual growth. You are attempting to transcend the physical body and establish a communication with the Higher Self when you develop your psychic talents. This is—and has always been—a natural part of our being.

Imagination, visual imagery, meditation, and self-hypnosis are keys to unlocking this magical part of your nature. You can create anything with your mind. When you transcend your physical self and tap into your Higher Self, you connect with the essence of the divine nature of the spiritual dimension.

Resist goal-oriented obsession with materialism. Spiritual awareness will not be attained by aggressive behavior. Resist the demand for instant enlightenment.

Psychic development is a gradual process. It is an awakening of gifts that are a natural part of your being. These talents have been denied and repressed by society. You have a responsibility to grow spiritually and psychically. The universe depends on it.

In metaphysics a merging of consciousness is emphasized. Some call this atonement. The material world stresses differences. You cannot do both. The differences observed on the earth plane are created by your mind. Apply discipline and open yourself to your Higher Self to bring these differences together.

Scientists estimate that people use no more than 10 percent of their brain. That leaves 90 percent of the mental function available for psychic abilities. Intuition, precognitive dreams, premonitions, telepathy, clairvoyance, and the other such experiences are but a small component of this untapped potential.

You face a challenge in developing your psychic abilities. The main mechanism is accessing the Higher Self. In the beginning of your training, you will be exposed to distorted and symbolic messages. Many of these communications remain in the subconscious. The techniques presented in this book are designed to overcome these blocks and free your natural abilities to send as well as receive psychic energy.

Questions concerning the nature of psychic phenomena persist, primarily because psychic experiences seem to lie outside conventional human experiences. Precognitive dreams are reported by about three-fourths of college students. The documented instances of precognition, telepathy, and other forms of psychic phenomena in everyday life are so numerous that they leave little room for doubt that these events do indeed occur. Telepathic communication occurs so frequently and is so widely reported that many consider it a normal part of daily interactions.

Expanding your psychic abilities demands that you reach beyond your five physical senses and everyday thought processes. This opens up a whole new world of potential experiences.

You can significantly increase your knowledge by developing your psychic talents. Absolutely everyone has the capability to do so using the exercises in this book. It involves transcending the physical body, but it is perfectly safe. Your potential for growth and knowledge is unlimited when you use these innate psychic gifts.

This is an important time in the history of our planet. A new age is here. A radical shift is in progress. Many people are achieving astounding results using these altered states of consciousness. Imagine what you can do by diligently working through this book.

The atonement I alluded to earlier was nicely expressed by the visionary Ralph Waldo Emerson. He firmly believed that the planet itself was a symbolic representation of the inner soul of man. In 1836 he published an essay entitled *Nature*. This work shocked the world because Emerson suggested that the earth itself was an expression of the same living spirit embodied in humanity. He instructed society to treat the land with the same respect shown toward people.

The twenty-first century represents the first full century of the Aquarian Age. Some predict that telepathic communication may become so commonplace it will be the normal means of interaction. It is possible to expand this concept and contemplate sending our very own brain waves off satellites!

Trust is a key element in psychic development. Learn to trust your inner self, your subconscious, and your Higher Self. Spiritual growth requires introspection. If you rely on the outside world and others, you will only be co-dependent and your psychic development will suffer.

The term "psychic" confuses many people. For some people it conjures up ESP and seeing the future. Others view it as an example of magic. Still others reject the concept because it does not fit into their preconceived definition of what is possible. Social conditioning shows in this confusion.

I refer to psychic phenomena as part of the "unseen or invisible world." Sometimes the term "unreal world" is used, because this universe is not detected by our five physical senses. Have you ever seen a mood, heard a gut feeling, tasted an emotion, or touched a dream? Our definitions are inaccurate because we are using the physical plane to describe phenomena that originate from the nonphysical dimensions.

Many of my patients and others inquiring at my Los Angeles office feel very drawn toward developing their psychic abilities. This is happening more and more frequently.

Your psychic abilities represent a world of unlimited potential. This multidimensional and multifaceted universe is just waiting for you to discover. By developing your psychic talents, you will greatly facilitate your personal enrichment and benefit the universe at the same time. This is psychic empowerment.

You do not need formal education to develop psychic gifts. By this I mean a college degree.

The meditations, self-hypnosis exercises, and visualizations presented here are merely tools. You are the best judge of what works for your own style. Try each exercise and select what feels comfortable and natural. Find the approaches that train you and enhance your life, making it richer, fuller, more exciting, and more enjoyable—both spiritually and materially.

The people around you will benefit from your psychic development. The flow of positive psychic energy you create will expand outward, changing not only you but the entire universe. Embrace your power, empower yourself and others, and use your gifts well and wisely.

Index

ABOUT THE AUTHOR

DR. BRUCE GOLDBERG graduated magna cum laude from Southern Connecticut State College in June 1970, earning a B.A. in biology and chemistry. He then attended the University of Maryland and School of Dentistry, receiving his Doctor of Dental Surgery degree in May 1974. Upon completion of a general practice residency program in dentistry, he set up both a general dental and a hypnosis practice. He retired from dentistry in 1989 and has since concentrated on his hypnotherapy practice in Los Angeles.

In 1984, Dr. Goldberg received his M.S. degree in Counseling Psychology from Loyola College.

The American Society of Clinical Hypnosis trained Dr. Goldberg in the techniques and clinical applications of hypnosis in January 1975. This organization trains only licensed dentists, physicians, and psychologists in the use of hypnosis.

Dr. Goldberg has appeared on many television and radio shows throughout the country. He has been interviewed on such shows as *Leeza, Donahue, Oprah, Joan Rivers, The Other Side, Regis and Kathie Lee, Tom Snyder, Jerry Springer, Jenny Jones, Montel Williams,* CNN, CBS *News,* and many others.

Through lectures, television, and radio appearances, and newspaper articles including interviews in *Time, The Los Angeles Times, and The Washington Post,* he has been able to educate many people about the benefits of hypnosis. He has conducted more than 33,000 past life regressions and future life progressions since 1974, and has helped thousands of patients empower themselves through the use of these techniques. In addition, Dr. Goldberg distributes cassette tapes to teach people self-hypnosis and to guide them into past and future lives.

Dr. Goldberg gives lectures and seminars on hypnosis and on regression and progression therapy, and on conscious dying as well; he is also a consultant to corporations, attorneys, and local and network media. His second book, *The Search for Grace,* was made into a television movie by CBS and first aired on May 17, 1994. Dr. Goldberg was the consultant on this film. His column, "Hypnotic Highways," appears in *Fate* magazine.

For information on self-hypnosis tapes, speaking engagements, or private sessions, Dr. Goldberg can be contacted directly by writing to:

Bruce Goldberg, D.D.S., M.S.
4300 Natoma Avenue
Woodland Hills, CA 91364
Telephone: (800) KARMA-4-U or (800) 527-6248
Fax: (818) 704-9189
Please include a self-addressed, stamped envelope with your letter.

BOOKS BY DR. BRUCE GOLDBERG
Past Lives–Future Lives
The Search for Grace: A Documented Case of Murder and Reincarnation
Soul Healing
Secrets of Self-Hypnosis